22247   MT
728
Page   P3

Playing String quartets

Date Due

PLAYING STRING QUARTETS

Playing String Quartets

Athol Page

LONGMANS

LONGMANS, GREEN AND CO LTD
48 Grosvenor Street, London W.1

Associated companies, branches and representatives
throughout the world

© *Athol Page 1964*
First published 1964

Made and printed in Great Britain by
William Clowes and Sons, Limited
London and Beccles

Contents

Author's Note

I am most grateful to all my friends who have helped in one way or another in the preparation of this book: to all those who have played quartets with me over the years, especially my colleagues in the New Manchester String Quartet and the members of what I might call our 'Haydn Quartet', who had quite a formidable task filling in the gaps in my knowledge of 'the 83'; to John Horton and Bernard Shore, who first gave me the idea of writing the book and who very helpfully read the galley proof and the typescript, respectively; to Paul Huband and Stephen Wilkinson, who greatly eased the burden of checking and obtaining facts. I am particularly grateful to Eileen Beattie and Harvey Phillips, who, apart from reading the typescript with a critical eye, have taught me more about chamber music in general than anybody else. Most of all I am grateful to my wife, who, far from objecting to the noises from which there is no escape in a musician's home, has always been encouragement itself.

Acknowledgements

We are grateful to the following for permission to include copyright material:

Oxford University Press for the poem *Severn Meadows* by Ivor Gurney and for a quotation from Sir George Dyson's *Fiddling while Rome Burns*; Stainer & Bell Ltd. for material from *Piano Quartet in A Minor* by Herbert Howells, and Universal Edition (London) Ltd. for material from *Fifth String Quartet* by Béla Bartók.

Probably the most ideal situation in which a musician can find himself is to be of equal gifts in a gifted string quartet. He shares the finest repertory in all music. There is no limit to the skill and artistry which he can contribute. And the audience to which a string quartet appeals is the most sensitive, receptive and discriminating that exists. Quartet and audience together are the aristocrats of music pure and unalloyed.

SIR GEORGE DYSON

Introduction

EVERYBODY knows that Haydn is the Father of the String Quartet. Allegri certainly wrote a quartet much earlier than this. Purcell also wrote 'string quartets', a medium he had to abandon later because Charles the Second so disliked fantasias for viols. The fact is, however, that the string quartet as it is known today did not emerge from this early chamber music, remotely beautiful though much of it is, but from the rough and tumble of Haydn's outdoor serenades.

Indirectly Emanuel Bach had a hand in it. How well he and Joseph Haydn would have got on together had they ever met! Emanuel's ill-concealed irritation with the vagaries of the flautist Frederick the Great might not have been the best of preparations for Joseph's long years of service to the baritonist Nicholas the Magnificent, but his approach to music would have delighted the younger man. ('I believe that music should, above all, touch the heart.') As it was, young Haydn met him only through his sonatas, which he played spellbound on a worm-eaten clavier in a bleak little garret across the square from the imperial palace in Vienna. The clavier was always used then to accompany music played indoors, but, when Haydn was doing a freelance job with one of those motley street bands of miscellaneous strings and wind, it had to be left behind. Not so the influence of Emanuel Bach. Through that influence he was steadily acquiring style, and his serenades and divertimentos soon made something of a stir, quite apart from that hilariously cacophonous serenade party at the Tiefer Graben bridge, for which he was chased by the police. Unlike the earliest chamber music these were not 'apt for voices or viols' but were apt for strings or wind. Gradually they became apt for strings alone, but even so not exclusively for a string quartet. Haydn's first divertimentos for an indoor quartet party, written in his early twenties, could equally well have been played by the orchestral strings. It was not until he had been employed by Prince Esterházy for some years that, in his middle thirties, he produced the first quartet which could not conceivably be played by anything except two violins, a viola and a cello. And it is anybody's guess whether that work is to be found in his Opus 3 or in his Opus 9.

But Haydn was a player as well as a composer. Across the face of that splendid clock in the Hoher Markt, the Ankeruhr, there move twelve majestic figures from Vienna's past, until finally, at noon, following the great Empress Maria Theresia, who had once had him whipped for climbing the palace scaffolding as a boy, comes Meister Joseph Haydn, violin and bow in hand. When he was suddenly cast adrift from St Stephen's Cathedral Choir he had little skill, and even in later years vowed that he was 'not a con- jurer' on the fiddle; but, as in everything else, he knew the value of a sound technique and arranged to have proper violin lessons as soon as he could afford them. There can be no doubt that these gave him an understanding of string playing which he could not otherwise have obtained, and no doubt an appreciation of a good instrument too. Haydn is the undoubted Father of the String Quartet, and has given us a wealth of music of which one can never tire, but for its grandfathers, for the players and the instruments, it is necessary to look back further still, to Corelli and Cremona.

It is not known if Corelli ever went to Cremona, but he certainly owned a Stradivarius violin, an instrument that later came into the possession of Salomon, the impresario who brought Haydn to London. He also used an instrument by Stainer, a highly talented Tirolese maker who, but for a life dogged by exceptional mis- fortune, might have become as great as any of the Italian masters. If Stainer was unlucky, Stradivarius was singularly fortunate. Cremona was the home of violin makers long before he was born. An ancient walled city, just south of the Bavarian Alps, between Venice and Milan, it had a population of about 10,000 in his day, with rising trade, several palaces maintained by the artistic nobility, and a cathedral which, whilst retaining the homeliness of a parish church, still rivals St Mark's, Venice, in the extravagance of its beauty. He was fortunate, too, in being apprenticed (the year after Corelli was born) to Nicolo Amati, the grandson of Andrea Amati, who made some of the earliest violins known to us today. The

Amatis, the most important violin makers in Cremona, were well-to-do and used only the best materials, a luxury that some fine craftsmen were unable to afford. They carefully selected the best pine for the belly, searching the forests of the Southern Alps, choosing trees that had developed slowly and evenly, tapping the trunks for resonance. The maple for the back, ribs and neck they bought in Venice, where large quantities were imported for building houses and making oars. Much of it was beautifully grained but brittle, as the Turkish timber merchants knew too well (the Venetian galley oars often broke, which was good for trade and helped the Turkish pirates too). But the wood was just what the Amatis needed and its marble grain still shines through the amber and the dragon's blood, the sandaric and turpentine, the aloe rubber, gamboge, campêche wood and mastic that went, one can only guess, into the making of their varnish.

Some twenty years later, when Stradivarius set up on his own, in the street in which most of the other violin makers lived, he could also buy the best materials. Unlike the Amatis he had not a private income and he sold his violins at a price which (even allowing for inflation) would be absurd today, but by working every weekday from dawn to dusk, hardly pausing for meals, he completed an instrument about once a week and made a comfortable living according to the standards of the time. Apart from his annual holiday in search of wood, he maintained this routine until well over ninety years of age, thus rivalling the astonishing output of contemporary artist-workmen in other spheres, painters, sculptors, silversmiths and musicians. On Sundays he went to the cathedral, where weekly recitals were given and new instruments tried out. Ruggieri, Gagliano, Bergonzi, Montagnana, and Guadagnini would probably have been there, though less frequently that wayward young genius Joseph Guarnerius. Afterwards, perhaps, sipping their wine in some open-air street-café nearby, they would listen respectfully to what Stradivarius had to say, freely discussing the secrets of their craft amongst themselves, although they would never reveal them to makers from other towns. All of them could play the instruments they made, so they were able to discuss things from the player's point of view. It is said that they delighted above all in the sonatas of Corelli, who, thus unknowingly inspiring them, contributed indirectly to the glory of their work. By the time he died the craft of violin-making had reached its peak and never, apart from the last magnificent instruments of Joseph Guarnerius, was it to reach such heights again. But the art of violin-playing, with Corelli himself as the first great master of the instrument, had only just begun.

Whilst still a young man Corelli was appointed to the court of Cardinal Ottoboni, a keen patron of the arts and a happy example of nepotism (he obtained his cardinal's hat only a few days after his uncle received the papal crown). The cardinal treated him less as servant than as friend, and his position became so assured that he once stopped the band in the middle of a performance to apologise sarcastically for interrupting his master's conversation with a guest. But his honoured position at court and the homage paid to him by illustrious foreigners visiting Rome did not turn his head. He appears to have been modest, unpretentious and thrifty (as Handel said of him, he liked nothing better than to gaze at pictures, which cost him nothing).

As a player Corelli had warmth rather than brilliance. He never felt at home beyond the third position and occasionally he met passages in the works of Handel and Alessandro Scarlatti that he could not play, but up to D''' his left hand technique was very sound. His bowing was 'firm and elegant' and his tone resembled a 'sweet trumpet'. It seems likely that he used vibrato (his pupil Geminiani lists the 'close shake', or vibrato, along with the traditional embellishments used for sustaining the interest of long notes) so he was one of the first players to discover that tone comes from the left hand as well as from the right. He never indulged in fireworks, as did some of his German contemporaries, but he impressed everyone with his taste and phrasing. His influence was great, far greater than that of a mere virtuoso, and his style became the model for violinists throughout Europe. With it went something of his musical integrity, in particular his insistence upon proper rehearsal before performance and clean ensemble playing, with all the players bowing up and down together. He was no more than human, however, and it is an encouragement to lesser mortals to know that he once made a careless mistake about his key signature, resolutely playing E naturals when the piece was in C minor and persisting in his mistake with such determination that it had to be pointed out publicly.

The Corelli tradition has always made technique the servant of artistry and has been handed on and developed through an unbroken line of great violinists, pupil and master in turn – Corelli himself – Somis – Pugnani – Viotti – Rode – Boehm – Joachim – and Leopold Auer, whose influence is still very much alive in Russia (though he left St Petersburg for New York in 1917), who taught several famous American violinists, and whose pupil, Isolde Menges, has brought inspiration to many string players in Britain. Corelli lives on and so, happily, does the Cremona tradition, maintained by numerous fine craftsmen throughout the intervening years. Without Corelli, Cremona and all that they represent, there might never have been that inexhaustible repertoire of string quartets available today, the foundations of which were laid by Joseph Haydn.

THE PLAYING

Technique

THE main requirement for playing quartets is the desire to do it. Four young men came back from the Second World War longing to do nothing else. Though not then expert on their instruments, they got together and began, learning, practising, rehearsing and gleaning the very best advice as if possessed. They were putting the cart before the horse and attempting the seemingly impossible, but they achieved it triumphantly, becoming an admirable professional quartet. In less exuberant times a more cautious approach is usual. Nothing is said at first about forming a regular quartet. Three others are invited to play once or twice for the fun of it. One of them, by tacit agreement, may not be invited again or may not want to come. There is no embarrassment on either side, as there can be if changes are left until firmer arrangements have been made, and sooner or later four players who get on and play well together will find themselves meeting regularly. Real passengers must be avoided, but the best individual players available do not necessarily make the best quartet. Age has not a great deal to do with it either, indeed there is a lot to be said for a combination of experience and youth. The most important things are to get on well together, to be prepared to work hard, and to play because one thinks there is nothing in music that quite comes up to playing string quartets.

EQUIPMENT

A lot is said about the importance of matching instruments. In one famous quartet the violins match so perfectly and are played

7

with such masterly similarity of style that one cannot tell which is
which. The main thing, however, is not that they should sound
alike but that all the instruments should blend. This, of course, is a
matter of degree, but the extremes, a strong modern instrument
amongst three mellow ones or a set of steel strings amongst gut,
should be avoided. In choosing an instrument, value for money must
be considered as well as tone. Instruments bearing the most famous
Italian names, if reliably guaranteed, have an antique value which
is almost certain to appreciate with time so they make a safe
investment, to say the least. Even Beethoven today, if given that
wonderful quartet of instruments again (Joseph Guarnerius –
Nicolo Amati – Vincenzo Ruggieri – Andrea Guarnerius), would
think twice about scratching a large B on the back of each and
leaving them lying carelessly about his room. (A Strad, incidentally,
is more difficult to play than some less sensitive instruments and
reveals its magic only to the finest players.) Instruments in the
middle price range are a more speculative buy, especially those with
minor Italian names, which are often priced beyond their intrinsic
worth. Before paying a fancy price it is therefore best to cast
snobbery aside and look round for something less glamorous,
perhaps even with a faked label, or without a name at all. By
searching deliberately for performance instead of pedigree one has
quite a chance of coming across an instrument that is every bit as
satisfying to play as a lesser aristocrat at three times the price.
A good bow is as important as the fiddle, indeed if both cannot be
bought at once it is best to go first for the bow. As a guide to the
young player prepared to put down the price of a motor cycle on a
better outfit, it would be sensible to spend not less than a quarter
of that sum on the bow.

Metal strings have such obvious advantages in tuning that they
are now very widely used. Their micro-adjusters make for great
accuracy; their fifths remain true; they hold their tuning well despite
changes of atmosphere. Moreover, on some instruments they add
strength and clarity to the tone. Unfortunately, although better
in most respects, they have a narrower expressive range than gut,
particularly lower down. The diehards therefore stick to gut,

although it causes them untold bother over temperature. Gut or metal, one should remember the advice of Mozart's father that 'the strings should be cleansed of all rosin-dust before one begins to play'.

The ornate brass mute of fifty years ago can still occasionally be seen, impressively obsolete. At the other extreme is the built-in mute requiring only a touch to slide it on. This is an immense convenience in the orchestra, but it can sound a little unconvincing on a solo instrument and sometimes buzzes slightly when not in use. For chamber music a pronged mute is preferable on the whole. Horn and wooden mutes break easily and have lost favour. The aluminium variety, which has a good tone and can be parked conveniently behind the ear, is the one most widely used today. It needs to be carefully adjusted to fit properly, having been known to fall off at awkward moments and even to defy a player trying to remove it in a hurry. Leather, though more expensive, has the same virtues as aluminium whilst having also a smoother tone and being the only mute which can be dropped without a clatter. No detachable mute, alas, is proof against forgetfulness, so some players attach theirs to the tailpiece with elastic, claiming that this gives them the best of both worlds. Whatever variety is selected, it is obviously desirable in the quartet to use mutes that are reasonably similar in tone.

One needs a high I.Q. to unfold a modern music stand and an even higher one to fold it up. Some players never seem to learn. Though it may tax one's intelligence, it is best to buy multi-jointed stands that fold up really small and can be adjusted really low. Suitable stands are not a luxury; besides being a great convenience, they make a difference to ensemble. When the same room is used regularly for rehearsals they can be left up semi-permanently, and then, human nature being what it is, a pencil should be tied to each.

TUNING

Accurate tuning is obviously fundamental but it is more difficult than it seems. It is also tedious, so one is tempted to skimp it.

The usual procedure is to ask if anyone has a reliable A, tune loudly and then practise an awkward passage in a remote key whilst the others are trying to listen to their fifths – it is only a rehearsal, after all. Unfortunately, performance finds one out. At the other extreme is the drill practised by one international quartet, as meticulously for rehearsal as for performance. They use a tuning fork, fairly sharp. (Most quartets tune sharp for brightness. A tuning fork can be sharpened, incidentally, by filing a little off the prongs and flattened, if too much is taken off, by filing down into the fork.) The viola stands the fork on his bridge whilst the cello very softly takes the A. This is the hardest part of the business and even experts are not ashamed to ask for help, it being easier to judge an A at a distance than close to the ear. His tuning completed, the cello takes over duty with the fork, and viola, second violin and leader tune in turn. The whole thing takes about ten minutes. Lesser mortals may not achieve quite such accuracy, but there can be no doubt that quiet individual tuning is the only satisfactory way. As a final check it is advisable for cello and viola to compare their C strings, since faulty intonation underneath does greater damage than it does on top. It is inadvisable, of course, to tune to harmonics, which ring false unless the string is absolutely true. If this initial tuning is given time to settle and the temperature plays no tricks, it should hold throughout a work. There should be no need, at any rate, for anything more than very slight unobtrusive adjustments between the movements.

INTONATION

Almost everybody has had trouble with intonation at one time or another, if not continuously, and more than one quartet that gives pleasure in the friendliness of the concert room has been less successful, through lapses of intonation, in the impersonal atmosphere of broadcasting. Playing in tune depends upon a good ear and accurate mechanical use of the fingers, neither of which is sufficient by itself but both of which help each other and can be improved. There is, alas, no easy road and no respite even when the goal has been attained. Casals once said that he could never play the scale of C in tune when starting his daily practice and that he had to get it right afresh each day. One's ear becomes more acute through careful listening and is helped by practising double stopping. The secret is not to blunt it by letting inaccuracies pass. Accurate fingerwork is obtained only through suitable exercises until each finger pattern is securely set. Obviously a good ear is useless if the fingers are not equal to the work, and the best mechanical fingering will go astray unless it is ceaselessly checked by ear. But, over and above the need for accurate intonation individually, it is essential that each player, by careful listening, should constantly adjust his intonation to that of the rest of the quartet so that even a temporary lapse by another player can be, as it were, absorbed. Slow, soft playing can help a lot and it is essential that the intonation should be soundly based. The cello has a great responsibility here and can probably do more than any other player to anchor the intonation as a whole. Thus, without being heavy, his playing should be firm. At the beginning of every rehearsal it is a good plan to tune in on something familiar and straightforward before tackling new or more difficult work, especially if the edge has been taken off the intonation by other playing since the quartet last met. In actual performance a wide vibrato can sometimes help in negotiating a doubtful patch, although this is not an expedient upon which undue reliance should be placed.

FINGERING

Other things being equal it is generally best, in quartets, to play in the first position, partly for security of intonation and partly for maximum length of string. Open strings are not objectionable, as they are when their effect is multiplied in the orchestra, and there is no need to make a habit of avoiding them, indeed their sound is sometimes preferable to that of the stopped note. Obviously, however, there are times when for particular tone quality or smoothness it is preferable to play in a high position on a lower string or to modify the open sound by using vibrato on a sympathetic stopped note (without actually bowing it), or on the nut of the fingerboard, on the open string itself.

It is unnecessary here to enlarge upon the usual maxims about fingering: shifting for preference at semitones; keeping a tidy hand set in the correct position, with fingers down well in advance for rapid playing; shifting cleanly, taking plenty of time; developing lively fingers by lifting briskly; attaining assurance through slow practice, only gradually increasing speed. These are things everyone learns in his lessons. He also learns, through scales, arpeggios and exercises, the safest and most economical fingering for covering the notes. This is extremely useful, especially in reading at sight and in rapid passage work, where well-established finger patterns make for certainty and speed. Sometimes, indeed, in modern music which reaches beyond the traditional techniques, it is advisable to think out finger patterns of one's own, so that those presto chromatic passages in the finale of Bartók Five, for instance, can be covered by a series of similar movements that are quickly learnt, in preference to a less systematic fingering. (Two short shifts, incidentally, are often more manageable than one longer one.) Occasionally something even more unusual may be required, as in that trying ostinato from the scherzo of Beethoven's last quartet, in which some cellists use their chin to stop the lowest note.

In slower, more expressive music it is phrasing, not economical coverage of the notes, that matters most. Imaginative fingering can make a tremendous difference to a tune, and it should always be thought out from the musical rather than from the technical point of view. Even if technically possible, a tune should rarely be played without any shifts at all. These need not induce the pronounced portamento that was fashionable in the days of the Lener Quartet; though done with more reserve they will still remove that element of dryness which is almost inseparable from the purely mechanical movement of the fingers up and down, helped by vibrato though it may be. Where they should be used depends entirely upon the tune itself, but the top note will very likely sound best if approached by shift and not by stretch. Having decided on the shifts, one must then fix the fingering leading up to them. Most players shift more confidently on certain fingers than on others, so it is worth some contrivance and adjustment to ensure that at these crucial points one is well placed for bringing them off as well as possible. Expression and expediency, unfortunately, conflict from time to time, and on these occasions it is worth reflecting that faint heart never won fair lady, nor yet a good tune either.

VIBRATO

Vibrato is sometimes looked on with suspicion, because it can be overdone. The fact is, however, that one has to work pretty hard to overdo it and that frequently it is not done enough. Players, knowing beforehand what they are trying to achieve, are prone to wishful thinking, their effects often being more apparent to themselves than to the less expectant listener. A vibrato which seems just right to the well-intentioned player can thus sound less convincing from outside. Generally speaking, therefore, it is best to go wholeheartedly for warmth, relying upon the candidness of the other players to point out if it is too much. It is also a sound general principle to make a habit of commencing the vibrato before the note is played, to ensure that it speaks immediately (particularly at the beginning of tunes), and also to continue the vibrato after the bow has left the string, especially in those endings where an 'orchestral cut-off' is inappropriate and it is desirable to 'leave an echo on the air'.

This is not to suggest that vibrato should be used indiscriminately or that it should be all alike. The wide, rich vibrato with bow well in the string that is required for many a tune of Brahms would be out of place in Fauré, Debussy or Ravel, where a more intense vibrato is usually needed, assisted by a lighter bow. In Schubert freedom of vibrato and lightness of bow are often both required. And there are times when no vibrato should be used at all, particularly in those wonderful moments in late Beethoven when a remote, disembodied sound is called for, as from some other world. In solo passages it is the spirit rather than the letter of the law that matters most. For example, in the beautiful Romance of Vaughan Williams's Quartet in A minor, *For Jean on her birthday*, the solo entries at the beginning, although marked senza vibrato, are played by Jean Stewart and Lorraine du Val (who, with the

other members of the Menges Quartet, gave the first performance)
'with just a nerve inside the note', their justification being that a
very little left hand is needed here to loft the tone and that the
composer himself, whenever they played the work to him for his
advice, was always more interested in the mood than in the means.
Chord passages, on the other hand, can often be most effective if
played with no vibrato at all. The last twelve bars of Schubert's
Death and the Maiden movement, for instance, sound haunting if
kept absolutely still – the hairpin in the last two bars can then be
achieved almost entirely with left hand alone.

BOWING

The first essential in bowing is to have a well-balanced bow with
a lively stick, and to screw it up not too tight. A tight bow greatly
limits variety of sound and is a common cause of insensitive tone.
The minimum tension that is practicable occurs when the hair just
begins to tighten on the stick. At that point, if the bow is correctly
held and used, the tone being 'drawn' rather than 'pushed' out, it
should be quite possible to get a tolerable legato tone. If this
cannot be managed reasonably well, then something is wrong either
with the playing or the bow. The best tension is certainly rather
more than this, but not much more. The better the bow, the less
it will need to be.

Occasionally, for spiccato playing, the bow can be a little tighter
than usual. Two contrasting examples may be quoted. First, from
the slow movement of the Dittersdorf E flat, where the under parts
accompany with this little bouncing figure, played pianissimo
towards the point.

Secondly from the scherzo of the Dohnányi D flat, where the solo
cello starts with this more prominent figure, near the heel.

Neither of these can be played without allowing the bow to bounce. That is necessary only very rarely, however. As a general rule it is always best to play with the bow on the string. This little chirrup from the finale of *The Bird*, for instance, would soon get untidy if allowed to bounce or if the bow was not quite ready on the string.

Every string player knows it is desirable to bow up and down together. This is partly for appearance and partly for sound. There are many passages where musically it does not matter in the least if the bowing is done opposite ways, and there is no danger of a mere string quartet approaching that ludicrous spectacle of the orchestra at one point in *En Saga*, where the violins with their contrary bowings seem to have gone completely mad. At the same time, it looks more businesslike to bow together, so it is worth doing so where possible, without making a fetish of it. There are many passages, on the other hand, where similarity of bowing is essential if there is to be similarity of sound. Generally speaking any tune or characteristic figure should be bowed in the same way by all the players and played in the same part of the bow. As an extreme example, it would sound quite wrong in the finale of *Death and the Maiden* for one player to play in the middle of the bow (even if he could keep it up) whilst the others were playing at the point (much the better bowing, of course).

The choice between down and up bows is dictated by practicability and by phrasing. Often a bowing which is awkward one way is much easier the other, especially if changes of string are involved. Sometimes it is easier to keep brisk repeated notes steady by playing them all up bow. A change of bow rather than a slur can help steadiness too. For instance, in the first movement of the Dittersdorf E flat, it is easier to play ♪ as marked in the score than ♪ as marked in the parts. Mostly, however, purely musical considerations must dictate the bowing. The better the player, the less difference will there be between his down and up, but the down bow will always tend to be the more suitable for tailing off a phrase and the up bow for leading into something else. The same applies to isolated notes, a down bow for those where a slight diminuendo is implied and an up bow for those which lead into the following rest. In the opening of *Death and the Maiden*, for instance, up bows (at the point) are needed before the rests, which are as dramatic as the notes themselves. An additional reason for playing the fourth beat of the first bar with a down bow is to enable the dotted minim to be held its full length.

Sometimes some other consideration conflicts with what would otherwise be the natural thing to do, so one has to compromise. For instance, in this figure from the first movement of *The Dissonance*, the second bar calls for a down bow, yet an up bow for the three preceding quavers can make them unduly prominent. Opinion thus differs as to which of these two bowings is best. The better the player, the more likely he is to select the bowing shown underneath the stave.

Slurs are often confusing, since it is rarely clear whether they indicate bowing or phrasing. Isolde Menges persuaded Vaughan Williams to indicate the phrasing in his Quartet in A minor by inserting dotted slurs as well as bowings, but few works are as clear as that. In quartets of the Viennese period many, if not most, of the slurs are editors' additions. Usually they are thoroughly playable, in accordance with sound nineteenth-century traditions, and provide a good basis upon which to work. For intensive rehearsal, however, it is worth looking up an Urtext score and thinking things out for oneself. In this connection it should be mentioned that when Beethoven writes ♩ ♩ ♩ ♩ the slur is not a bowing but an indication, in accordance with the convention of the time, that the notes are to be just separated, not played short. Quite often, of course, this may be the most suitable bowing too, indeed leisurely repeated notes, as in the slow movement of *The Dissonance*, almost always sound best if played two or more to a bow.

Range of tone colour needs to be as wide as possible and is affected by the part of the bow that is used, by distance from the bridge, by pressure and by speed. Of these, pressure, although perhaps the most obvious, is probably the least effective of them all. At the pianissimo extremes one must guard against wispy, one-hair bowing that has no substance in it. Leopold Mozart said years ago that 'by no means are they to be praised who express piano so softly that they can scarce be heard; one must always play firmly'. In classical quartets there must always be tension in the tone, so one cannot relax the pressure overmuch. Instead, softness must be achieved by playing nearer the point, bowing further from the bridge and slowing up the bow. This wonderful passage from the slow movement of the Beethoven F minor illustrates the need for tension in the softest playing.

At the fortissimo extreme we have this, from the first movement of the same work.

To play it effectively is rather like forcing a locked door. Pushing against it, however heavily, will do no good; one must stand right back and kick. Similarly, pressing hard into the string will only make this passage rasp. Here also, one must stand right back, bowing firmly from the shoulder, with not much pressure downwards, but at the heel, near the bridge and with a very speedy bow. If pressure is the least effective of the variants in bowing, speed is the most valuable. Once again it is useful to consider the extremes. In the slow movement of the Schubert Quintet in C the middle parts start as follows, with an approximate metronome mark of ♪ = 76 and proceed one bow to a bar, a veritable slow bicycle race.

It would make it much easier to change the bow in the middle of the bar, and a skilled player could do so unobtrusively enough. The increased speed, however, would quite dispel the atmosphere, turning a wonderfully rarified sound into something more commonplace. Similarly, in the climax of Samuel Barber's Adagio, it is tempting to cope with the fortissimo by taking extra bows, but they reduce the tension of the music correspondingly, and eliminate that element of struggle which is often the very essence of a climax. At the other extreme, speed of bow can give great vitality to the tone whilst keeping it light and buoyant. A sluggish bow makes for dull playing, especially underneath, and most players could afford to speed it up. A great deal can be learnt from Haydn minuets, so simple, so varied and so fresh.

PIZZICATO

For many years the scherzo of the Ravel Quartet was the standard example of pizzicato with a vengeance. It has now been superseded by the delicious allegretto pizzicato of Bartók Four. Anybody who has mastered that movement knows nearly all there is to know about pizzicato playing—but not quite everything. It would not equip him, for instance, to play the deceptively simple second cello part in the slow movement of the Schubert Quintet, which can all too easily drag back to earth that heavenly sound suspended up above.

The majority of players have never practised pizzicato thoroughly but have simply picked it up. Most players could learn something from the more systematic fingerwork of the guitarist, especially in the use of two fingers for running passages and in playing chords. Two-finger pizzicato, unfortunately, calls for much slow practice, on exercises as well as on the pieces to be played, if it is to be an improvement upon an agile first finger alone, as it can become in time. Chord playing, on the other hand, can be improved more easily. The guitarist normally plucks the notes of his chords simultaneously, using thumb as well as fingers, pinched inwards. This produces a clean, crisp sound and is not particularly difficult to do. Often it is preferable to the commoner method on the violin of striking across the strings, however rapidly that may be done. Nowadays composers realise the variety of sound obtainable from pizzicato, and Bartók is quite specific in indicating how his chords are to be played—non arpeggio, arpeggio ↓ or arpeggio ↑. Ravel marks some of his three-note chords quasi arpa and others simply fortissimo, the inference being that the latter are to be played non-arpeggio. Debussy gives no indication at all. Where the player has nothing else to go on, as he rarely has in music before 1900, he must therefore decide on one of these alternatives for himself—and usually the context provides him with a reliable guide.

A well-covered hammer on the pianoforte makes a rounder note than one that is thin and worn. The same is true of pizzicato fingers—the more meat the better. For single notes the second finger is therefore often preferable to the first, and sometimes, for maximum tone, it is best to use both fingers simultaneously. (The exact placing of pizzicato notes is more difficult than it seems, especially when soft and slow; they are more easily controlled by drawing a flat finger across the string than by plucking with a crooked finger away from the fingerboard; for pianissimo chords, as at the end of the scherzo of the Debussy, it is merely necessary to lift the finger quickly off the string, without plucking it at all.) Distance from the bridge makes a considerable difference to the tightness or looseness of the sound, as well as to the length of time the note will ring. A note plucked near the middle of the string has more buoyancy than one plucked near the end and is generally preferable, but sometimes a drier, more percussive sound is required, indeed Walton actually marks some of his pizzicato secco, whilst Bartók goes so far as to direct sul ponticello. Such exceptions apart, the most important factor in pizzicato tone is unquestionably vibrato. It lifts the notes off the ground and should invariably be used unless there is some good reason to the contrary.

Two minor points may be mentioned last. First, experienced players usually discard their bow when there is an opportunity to pick it up again in time, since holding it adds to the difficulty of awkward pizzicato – in the celebrated Haydn *Serenade* it would be merely a convenience but in Bartók Four a necessity. Secondly, the difficulty of those sudden changes back to arco can sometimes be overcome by left hand pizzicato (particularly if the last note is an open string) or by shifting glissando to the final note, instead of actually plucking it (the only alternative for the cello at one point in *The American*).

ENSEMBLE

In almost every quartet the first and second violins sit side by side, their instruments facing outward, but opinion varies as to where the viola and the cello should be placed. Most quartets have a decided preference one way or the other, claiming that they cannot attain such good ensemble if seated differently. If in doubt, both arrangements should be given a reasonable trial. One of them will almost certainly seem better than the other and one should then stick to it. Either way, the inside players should face slightly towards the audience, partly for blend of sound and partly so that each player can see the others easily. For similar reasons, the stands should be placed as close together as freedom of playing will allow and should be adjusted really low – the double-sided mahogany antique, complete with candlesticks and inset lyre, may add to the attractions of the music room, but it is not for playing string quartets.

Quite a lot of ensemble has to be attained by eye; indeed at one point in the Mendelssohn Octet, submerged in a spate of swirling scales, one's only hope is to watch the other players' bows. That is an extreme example, and for the most part it is only necessary to look out for leads. With increasing experience of playing together these can be given almost imperceptibly, yet clearly enough to be picked up from the corner of one's eye. It is a good plan for all the players to practise them in a mirror, until it becomes as easy to give an unobtrusive lead as not. The main thing, although it is easier said than done, is to know precisely what one intends to do, particularly where setting a tempo is concerned. The second violin who can carry the viola neatly with him in those eight repeated quavers in the first bar of *The Bird* has learnt his lesson very well indeed. Endings have to be tidy too – sometimes they receive less care than beginnings – but one must beware of finishing with a jerk. A cut-off from the leader is rarely needed and it is usually enough to watch for the finish of his bow.

Although the eye is often useful for ensemble, it is, of course, the ear that is most important. Critical listening improves with practice, like everything else, and, although it may bring with it disquieting revelations, it brings also the infinite satisfaction of accompanying and fitting in. One needs to develop an ear that will function independently of technique and that will not switch off when difficulties of notes arise. This is clearly fundamental, but is a great deal harder than, to the uninitiated, it might seem to be. Nobody ever achieves quite the degree of objective listening he desires, but every player's ear, by constant striving for small points, becomes gradually more vigilant. He can then accompany, instead of counting doggedly, and the playing, although flexible, begins to fit. Some music, indeed, can only be played 'by ear'. It is quite impossible, for instance, to 'count' the scherzo of Bartók Five at speed. In this sort of music, as in a Mendelssohn scherzo also, the only way is to relax and play entirely by sound, anticipating the entries slightly in order to compensate for that time-lag which nobody, however quick, can entirely overcome and trusting that merciful providence, reinforcing previous practice, will do the rest.

Apart from keeping together, the main problems of ensemble are joins, balance and texture. The smoothness of joins can often be improved by taking in the note immediately preceding or following one's own, either mentally, or by fingering them silently, or even by just touching them with the bow. There is a particularly awkward join in the minuet of Rasoumovsky Three, where a solo scale is passed from violin to viola and to cello and where some kind of overlap is essential if smoothness is to be achieved. Sometimes a tune is passed from part to part and then it is necessary to think of the phrasing as a whole. Perhaps the best known example comes from the Schumann Piano Quintet. Schumann phrases the viola and cello separately, but it improves the shape to think of the tune as a single four-bar phrase.

Only modern composers have made much use of dynamic markings as a guide to balance, and dynamics, in any case, are entirely relative so there is still no escape from balancing by ear. A tremendous lot can be learnt from the first two chords of Rasoumovsky Three.

Half an hour spent in balancing these will achieve far more than many hours of less critical playing, and there are countless passages in the quartets of every period where the lessons of these two chords can be applied. Often, however, the principal interest is in one part, the others having to accompany. This should not be too inhibiting. If one knows what to listen for and hears it clearly, that will usually be enough. Accompaniment must always give support, and it does not help the principal player of the moment to leave him high and dry, as inexperienced accompanists are sometimes apt to do. Indeed, where a full-blooded tune is concerned it is often better for the player himself to work harder to get it through than for the others to fade away. Many quartet tunes, in fact, require as much playing as those of concertos, and it is sometimes a good pre-liminary (since it is mistaken self-indulgence to practise the tunes themselves too much) to open out on something else that is even bigger still. This does not, of course, mean simply playing loud but projecting the tone so that it really carries.

Balance is inseparable from texture and the main need here is to let in plenty of air. Quartet playing should rarely sound thick but should always have bite and colour. It is a great mistake to play the notes too literally. A steady, monotonous tone may occasionally be needed for some particular effect, but in general it is the last thing that is wanted. Every phrase and every little snatch of accompaniment must be made to talk, with as much articulation and emphasis and rise and fall as an animated conversationalist puts into his voice. It is impossible for the composer to mark in all the little accents and hairpins, the precise note-values and the expressive notes that he requires. These have to be supplied by the player – therein lies the fascination of playing string quartets. If he supplies them freely and with imagination, his playing will have vigour without becoming thick. Many little points of balance will then be naturally resolved, the texture being transparent, not opaque.

REHEARSAL

Before the Kolisch Quartet began the rehearsal of a new work each player learnt his own part by memory from the score. That is thoroughness carried to the extreme. Most players, if convinced that this was a necessary preliminary, would never play a string quartet again. Their method does, however, illustrate two cardinal principles, that serious rehearsal is a waste of time unless everyone takes the trouble to learn his notes, and that all the players should know the score. In point of fact, very detailed private practice can often do more harm than good until a reasonable idea has been obtained of the work as a whole, since one may get preconceived ideas individually, of bowing and the like, which are difficult to reconcile afterwards. It is usually best to set the general shape first, and that can be done only by playing each movement through until its design is clear. This is not to suggest that nothing should be done before the first play through. A glance at the score is invaluable beforehand, particularly if one is looking for musical rather than technical points. A useful exercise is to play through the whole of a movement on one's own instrument, following the tune from part to part. Not all music lends itself to this treatment, but it is surprising how much does. One can get a good idea in this way, for instance, of the first movement of the Ravel or the Walton Quartet and, by confining oneself to the melodic line, can obtain a clearer conception of the flow of the music than by score reading at the piano.

Perhaps the main requirement for detailed rehearsal is that everyone should feel absolutely free to have his say and should bear no resentment at any criticism of himself. One of the most valuable assets any player can have is friends who will tell him the bare unvarnished truth, and thanks, not excuses, make the best reply to any suggestion about his playing. A good rehearsal, however, need not be a free-for-all and in some quartets a courteous custom develops of making comments through the leader. ('Peter, don't you think that Paul is rushing it a little here?') It takes time for such an atmosphere of friendly comment to develop but, once established, it makes a tremendous difference both to the pleasure and the effectiveness of rehearsal.

Detailed rehearsal involves taking the music to pieces, and it is essential, having done so, to put it together again by a straight play through at the end. Taking it to pieces can be done in several ways, and, since one of the objects is to expose mistakes, it is best done in a room not too resonant for clarity. Some passages can be usefully practised in pairs. For intonation, soft slow practice is invaluable, whatever the actual markings may be – it gives one time to listen really intently. Slow practice is also occasionally useful for ensemble (technique, of course, should be practised individually at home). Music loses its character, however, if taken at too incorrect a speed, so beyond a certain point one ceases to practise the difficulty usefully. A more effective and realistic method is to practise in short sections nearly up to speed and to fit them together as one goes along. This is particularly useful with difficult modern music, which tends to go in at one ear and out at the other if tackled in sections too lengthy to retain. Practising to a metronome is seldom desirable, but just occasionally it may act as a salutary reminder of what a steady tempo should be. In that awkward little scherzo of Beethoven's Opus 18, No. 6, for instance, even the best quartets sometimes run away.

Making the most of rehearsal time depends upon what one is trying to achieve. Generally speaking, amateur quartets mostly read works through, thus becoming acquainted with a wide repertoire, whilst professionals confine themselves to a few works each season which, by intensive rehearsal, they try to bring as near perfection as they can. Most amateurs would improve considerably and gain more satisfaction in the end if they were to rehearse in greater detail than they do. Over a period of a month or two, one work at least should be practised thoroughly, alongside those that are played straight through. On the other hand, should intensive practice ever take the sparkle, for instance, out of Haydn – a common danger with professionals – it is a good plan to play straight through one of his unfamiliar quartets just for the fun of it.

Coaching is stimulating now and then. An outsider can hear many things which the players themselves may miss, and fresh ideas on the music are always enlivening, whether one agrees with them or not. A tape recorder is also useful occasionally. In addition to technical imperfections, intonation particularly, it will probably show that still more space might be taken in order to make the phrasing clear. In unskilled hands, however, it can be misleading about tone and balance, and it can waste an appalling lot of time.

PERFORMANCE

Nobody can claim to know a quartet really well until he has performed it to an audience. Performance brings an intensity of awareness which no amount of rehearsal or passive listening can supply. Flaws of technique are unexpectedly revealed but, more important still, the shape of the work is thrown into relief so that, alongside the immediacy of playing, one suddenly sees it more clearly as a whole. One seems, in a curious way, to be both more detached as well as more absorbed than in rehearsal, to be both inside and outside the music simultaneously, and to acquire a heightened appreciation of the work itself. The performance need not be a very grandiose affair. Just a few friends gathered in the music room at home will do (the pleasantest setting of all, indeed, for quartets). But in one way or another, in public or in private, and however modest one may be, performance must be faced if the music is to be fully known and understood.

Nerves affect nearly everybody, so one is in good company. There is no cure and they do not improve much with the years. Some of the greatest players, in fact, have been afflicted with agonies of nervousness after a lifetime of experience on the concert platform. It is just one of the hard facts of life that must be accepted, even welcomed, for without nerves many performances would be dull. Fortunately quartets are a corporate responsibility, and it is steadying to sense that another of the team is nervous too and needs support, though as far as possible nerves should be kept to oneself and not discussed.

It is one thing, however, to suffer nerves knowing that the work has been learnt thoroughly and quite another to feel apprehensive because it has been insufficiently rehearsed. That awkward little solo in the last movement, which one had meant to master but had left too late, can all too easily cloud everything that goes before. There is unfortunately no substitute for learning the notes.

Playing quartets is hard work, and by the third of them one may begin to tire. A good meal, though it may be difficult to swallow, helps one to last out. It is essential to have a green room, even at semi-social functions. Nothing is worse than trying to make polite conversation before having to play, and, in any case, there must be somewhere to tune properly. This must be got absolutely right before going on, and it is a good plan, both in order to give the strings time to settle and to adapt the playing to the hall, to get there early and play through a few contrasting passages, though not too many, before the audience arrives. The more resonant the room, of course, the slower the tempos one can afford to take. If very resonant, it helps to play on a carpet. If dead, one must grade up the dynamics and sit in front of the best sound-reflecting surface that can be obtained.

On the platform itself everything possible should be done to give an impression of calm, not least because it helps to quieten the nerves. A brief word to the audience about the music will often break the tension and introduce that companionable note which is the essence of chamber music (indeed this might well be done sometimes at public concerts as well as at those in private). Apart from this, all distractions should be eliminated, so that the audience can concentrate on the music rather than the players. Stands and chairs should have been properly set out beforehand and unobtrusive pizzicato tuning practised, so that any minor adjustments required between movements need not rudely break the spell. The players should avoid excessive movement in their playing, partly for the look of it and partly because controlled playing is more concentrated and efficient. Even little domestic problems such as turning over must be arranged in advance and not left to the luck of the moment (it is surprising how often the first note after a hurried turn contrives to be an awkward one to get). Nobody can turn over satisfactorily in the César Franck Quartet, which goes on for pages with barely a rest at all, but in most music it is possible to get round the difficulty in one way or another. A few bars can be written out, or another player may be free to turn or take in an extra note, as the second violin does in both cases in the Dohnányi

D flat. Two copies can sometimes be used (there is a lot to be said, on other grounds also, for possessing separate copies as well as bound volumes of the standard works). But the simplest method, and one that works quite frequently, is to cut the page so that the top half can be turned before the bottom half is played. It is rarely satisfactory to gain time by slowing up the music, as first violins have been known to do in that vital bar preceding the last of the *Death and the Maiden* variations.

Programmes have to be considered both from the playing and from the listening point of view. The advice once given by a well-known quartet player was 'Never start with *The Lark*.' It is certainly inadvisable, unless supported by plenty of experience, to begin with exposed playing requiring particular nicety of judgement, such as the opening of *The Lark* demands. If there are any doubts at all, the first work should be chosen with an eye to settling down, and something entailing straight, clean playing will probably be best. For the rest, one should aim at variety. Modern music should be considered first, as it is apt to get overlooked. Less than two centuries ago it was contemporary composers who provided the music everybody played. Nowadays, with so many well-tried works conveniently at hand, the contemporary composer is not so indispensable. Even if published, his quartets may lie hidden in some catalogue, so one has to search them out. That is no excuse for quartet players to remain more than one generation behind the times. Their searchings will be rewarded by discovering quite a lot of modern music that is much more playable and engaging than it may seem to be at first. Modern music is also practical politics. Nobody would deliberately treat a modern work less conscientiously than a classic or seek to shield behind its unfamiliarity, but there is no doubt that it can be easier to get away with Hindemith, for example, than with Haydn. Sometimes, instead of a full-length work, one might play a shorter piece or two, such as Schubert's *Satz*, Wolf's *Serenade* or Turina's *La Oracion del torero*. There is no reason, either, to stick too rigidly to the comparatively recent convention of playing a work complete or not at all. A Mendelssohn scherzo, or Vaughan Williams's beautiful Epilogue from his quartet *For Jean on her birthday*, or Samuel Barber's celebrated Adagio in its original setting, stand well on their own. There are several volumes of encore movements, some of which might be considered for the programme proper, and there are also the attractive Russian pieces entitled *Les Vendredis*. It is sometimes interesting to play two separate movements for comparison, such as the first movements of Beethoven Opus 95 and Bartók Five, so different in a way and yet so similar in their uncompromising, headstrong drive. A complete change of colour is refreshing also. At professional quartet concerts the cost of an extra player can be prohibitive, but in private the chance of performing, say, the Mozart Clarinet Quintet should not be missed. For the principal standard work one must balance the claims of well-worn favourites like the Borodin, the Dohnányi, or Dvořák's *The American* with those of the major classics. Generally speaking, the greater the music the easier it is to give a satisfying if not an impeccable performance. Great music shines through technical imperfections as lesser works do not. Beethoven's A minor, for instance, requires far more understanding than his Opus 18 No. 2 in G (a most exacting work to play) but technical faults are much more readily pardoned and ignored. Many players have more understanding than they have technique and would be quite mistaken to assume, through diffidence, that the greatest quartets are not for them. But, like the best of everything, great music is not come by easily.

Interpretation

A T the beginning of the *Beethoven Quartets*, Volume I, the very first notes are these,

Beethoven took infinite pains to fashion this little fragment into a satisfying shape, starting from this loose, rudimentary idea.

Interpretation is somewhat similar. It is also, within much narrower limits than composition, a search for shapes that satisfy. These are cast by the composer first, but the performer has to give them final definition. He must perceive the shape the composer had in mind and then chisel it. Perhaps he may give emphasis to certain notes or hold back a little to allow the climax time to tell. Beethoven was aiming for precisely these two points when moulding this poignant phrase from Rasoumovsky One.

The performer cannot change his notes and is confined entirely to small adjustments of his time and tone. Compared with the composer this does not seem much to do, yet it is vital. By its very subtlety, too, it can fascinate a player all his life and give him, through constantly working within such narrow limits, an unusually well-developed sense of spacing and of emphasis. Good music invariably makes sense and, to those who can think logically in time and tone, its shapes become increasingly obvious. Casals, to the inspiration of so many, has considerably increased his masterly perception of these things since reaching sixty years of age.

In music, as in other things, understanding does not usually come in a sudden flash of inspiration, but through careful study of the text. Some great performers, renowned for their revealing interpretations of the classics, have claimed that they do no more than play what the composer wrote. That is olympian understatement, to say the least, but there is some truth in it. They perceive the shapes of music with greater clarity than most, from simple phrasing to the structure as a whole. Because the shapes are clear, not blurred or warped, their underlying meaning is revealed more clearly too. This brings emotional understanding which, in performance, adds a glow of passionate conviction to the final burnishing of the work, whilst keeping it faithfully in shape. Fortunately, perhaps, composers do not tell everything. They still leave the interpreter to make his own translation of the text. But they annotate it pretty fully and offer hints that are often very broad indeed.

The broadest hint is usually the precise value of the notes themselves. The opening of the slow movement of Schumann's Piano Quintet, for instance, depends entirely upon obsessional exactitude of notes Schumann, like Schubert before him, used inflexibility to picture lread. The music has a fixed, hypnotic stare which any relaxation of tempo, tension or note values will immediately break,

molto p ma marcato

In Beethoven, though with a contemplative tone, the same exactness of notes portrays serenity. To bring repose, the viola needs very steady rhythm here (Opus 95, slow movement) with semi-quavers that are absolutely even, the first of them being as long as the second. (Snatching the first note of a duplet is one of the commonest of rhythmic errors.)

In some performances of *The American* (first movement) the figure repeatedly assails the listener. In actual fact it is written this way only once, at a climax, appearing elsewhere as . Dvořák is asking for melodic, not percussive playing here. These are just three examples, from an almost infinite number which might be quoted, in which precise note-values will accurately fix the shape and lead to realisation of the mood.

Accentuation is another important clue, and it is just as necessary to avoid it where it is not marked as to put it in where it is. Schubert was sometimes careless about phrase marks but hardly ever about accents. This tune from *Death and the Maiden* can therefore be taken at its face value. There is no accent on the third beat and, if one is permitted to creep in, Schubert's mood of lilting resignation is at once dispelled.

Where, too, could one find a broader hint to lighten the first beat of the bar than in this tune from his great G major Quartet?

Sometimes, where no indication is given, a clue to accentuation may
be found in another part. At the end of Mozart's Quartet in D
minor, K.421, for instance, it may not be clear to the individual
player of ♪♪♪ | ♪ whether the stress should come before or
after the bar-line. It settles it, however, to know that another player
has ♪ | ♪.

Accents, dynamics and other markings must be interpreted in context, of course, and in accordance with the custom of the composer
himself and the conventions of the time. The Viennese composers
give only >, whilst in Dvořák there are the additional refinements
of ∧ and –. On the other hand, even within one movement,
Beethoven marks >, tenuto, sforzando and rinforzando, a wide
range of alternative accentuation. In Mendelssohn and Schumann
the > is nearly always bright; in Brahms it is usually dark, with
a lean on the note rather than a stab. Dynamics are largely relative.
It is not much use seeing the marking mezzoforte, for example,
unless one realises at the same time that the other parts are marked
no more than piano. Short of endless inquiry among the players
only the score will indicate this. Crescendos should always be
interpreted more faithfully, if anything, at their climax than at
their beginning. It is the final spurt that counts. Sometimes, if the
crescendo is very long, it is justifiable to delay starting it or to drop
down at some suitable point in order to build up again, as one does
four bars before the triple forte at the end of *The American*.

Repeats are used simply to avoid writing out the same passage
twice. As often as not the music should go straight on as if that had
been done, in minuets especially, so that the listener is unaware
of the double-bar. A device frequently found in Haydn and
Mozart is the sudden drop from forte to piano, often on the
bar-line. Composers at that time were accustomed to the Corelli
bow, which, with its wider gap between hair and stick, took
appreciably longer to bite the string than do our bows today.
There was thus no alternative, after a sudden release of
pressure, but to leave a tiny gap before starting the next phrase,

and there is thus no need, at the present day, to rush straight on. Trills, in the seventeenth century and before, did not go off like electric bells but were regarded as melodic ornamentations of the note. Even today they might have a wider range of expression than they are sometimes given. On occasion one needs a very rapid trill indeed, but not always by any means. Staccato marks are also subject to a wide variety of interpretation. In Beethoven's day it was an accepted convention that ♪ ♪ ♪ ♪ indicated notes of about three-quarters length, only just detached and not necessarily taken in a single bow, that ♪ ♪ ♪ ♪ indicated notes of about half their written length and ♪ ♪ ♪ ♪ a short, sharp staccato of quarter-length notes or less. Beethoven was always insistent that his copyists should not write a dot for a dash or vice versa, but in modern editions that distinction is no longer made, so the player must use his own discretion. Perhaps the composer with the least variety of staccato length is Brahms. There is not one really short staccato in any of his string quartets.

Correct tempo is the most important requirement in interpretation, so Toscanini said – he possessed such remarkable conviction of tempo that his performances of the same symphonic movement, though timed at intervals of several years, often differed only a second or two in their total length. In modern music, metronome marks give a useful guide. Bartók even adds a timetable at the end, $24\frac{1}{2}$ seconds up to letter A, and another 22 up to letter B. It is as though he is standing over the players, aloof and uncompromising, stop-watch in his hand. Composers themselves, however, often depart from their own metronome marks in performance, so they presumably intend their players to use a little discretion too. Obviously their markings should be taken seriously, yet not followed so meticulously as to become more of a hindrance than a help. Beethoven's metronome marks are frequently unreliable. He added them, with great enthusiasm for Maelzel's new invention, after he had become too deaf to hear the results. Usually the best evidence of tempo comes from the music itself, the time signature and the

Italian terms. The beautiful slow movement of Haydn's Quartet in
D, Opus 76 No. 5, for instance, is sometimes taken so slowly that
it plods, adagio $\frac{4}{4}$. It is actually marked largo (which is considerably faster than adagio – Purcell called largo a 'middle tempo')
and the time signature is ₵. These two facts combined should
give a sufficient clue to its enchanting, leisurely swing, and if
further evidence is required one need only turn to the repeated
crotchet chords which are a particular feature of the accompaniment
later in the movement. It is inconceivable that Haydn would have
written anything as monotonous as this except to serve some
rhythmic purpose – and it is quite impossible to achieve that purpose
unless the tempo has adequate momentum.

In connection with this last passage it should be remembered that
the seventeenth-century convention of playing 𝅘𝅥𝅮. 𝅘𝅥𝅯 as 𝅘𝅥𝅮.. 𝅘𝅥𝅰 did
not suddenly cease by imperial decree on 31 December 1699. It
took more than another century for it to die a lingering death. Thus,
if the first violin is prompted to give edge to the rhythm by
lengthening his dotted notes, he will not be flouting the composer's
wishes; he will be expressing them. (On the other hand, in com-
pound time, it was the convention to play this figure so that the
semiquaver coincided with the third quaver of each beat. This
convention also died slowly and there are several passages in
Beethoven and Schubert, especially in works with piano, where it
still seems best to follow it.)

Unfortunately, although other conventions come and go, nobody
has yet found a satisfactory alternative to the convention of writing
music down in bars. Poetry has happily escaped. One of the
most dispiriting of all effects in music is the dogged thump of the

first beat in the bar. It is at its worst in ♪ | ♩ ♪♩ ♪ | and here, as in many other figures in compound time, it can be helpful to hinge the rhythm to the final quaver (a down-bow on this quaver is usually implied). Lightening unimportant first-beats, in fact, is always one of the most necessary things the performer has to do. Beecham, by his gestures, did this constantly; he never 'carved'.

The other great trouble is the bar-line. The tendency is to see it coming and rush at it. This, also, is most disquieting. Music needs time to breathe and, in Brahms especially, it is over the bar-line that it usually seems to need it most. It needs every bit of time available and sometimes even a little more; indeed, rather than starve the bar-line, it is often better to borrow from the middle of the bar. This can usually be done only with the instinctive help of another player. For instance, in a rhythm such as ♩. ♩ | ♩, it is impossible to take the necessary space if the accompanying player has been sluggish over 𝄾 ♩ ♩ 𝄾 | 𝄾. It is not a slowing down that is needed but a sense of vitality combined with spaciousness. In ♩. ♪♩ | ♩. (Trio: *Death and the Maiden*) the second violin actually anticipates the bar-line slightly in order to give the others space to play ♩. | ♩ ♩ ♩. This is not as contradictory as it might seem, the music having two-bar phrases which could equally well have been written in $\frac{6}{4}$, minus the bar-line as shown here.

An underlying flexibility of rhythm is implicit in all music, although it cannot be indicated in detail in the score, and it is the most important contribution to performance that the player has to make. Rhythm can be metronomic, or it can lean forward on its tempo, or back on it. Sometimes, as in those closely clinging rhythms of Brahms, it can have a two-way pull, so that one player is urging forward as another is holding back. Sometimes, as in many of Schubert's tunes, it is completely relaxed, flowing on regardless as though it were thinking of something else. Beecham was the supreme master at standing aside and letting the music play itself. Metronomic rhythm (as distinct from relaxed, 'musikant' rhythm) is comparatively rare. An instance from Schumann has already been quoted. Schubert uses it to picture horror, relentlessness and vacancy of mind. Bartók actually marks one passage 'mechanico' in his Fifth Quartet – it sounds like a mocking, stiff-jointed marionette. It is one thing, however, to turn the handle or maintain a rigid rhythm deliberately and quite another to do so because one cannot think of anything else to do. Unless there is some good reason to the contrary, music always has a forward or a backward pull and its vividness depends very largely upon how well the constant little adjustments of rhythm are made. In general, Beethoven's tunes move decisively towards their cadences, whereas those of Brahms have a rhythmic drag towards the end. This is no more than might be expected from what is known of the composers themselves. The unsettled, vacillating rhythms sometimes found in Schubert and Schumann could be explained in a similar way. Rhythm, in fact, is almost always veering to and fro. A particularly striking and delightful example is found in the opening tune of the finale of Shostakovich's Piano Quintet. It begins with a ritardando on its first beat (surely this must be unique?), sways uncertainly and then gradually gathers momentum, rather jerkily. It is like a clown, slightly tipsy, rocking genially on his feet and lurching unsteadily into a trot.

Most of the points discussed already have been concerned with details of phrasing. A phrase does not make a string quartet, but in good music the different phrases often have striking homogeneity, so work done on one is widely applicable elsewhere. It is important to get the details clear not only for their own sake but so that they can be left, so to speak, to play themselves, whilst the players take a longer view. Bifocal vision is required, long sight as well as short. Generally speaking, the more that flexibility of detail is achieved, the steadier the over-all shape can be. Joins, in any structure, are always the hardest things to do, and that is where music, unless it is firmly put together, is most liable to creak. Many second subjects, for instance, feel as if they should go slower than the first and, in performance, they should certainly sound as if they do. As far as possible, however, this should be an illusion rather than a fact, contrived from the way the tune is played. If the basic tempo is actually changed it will almost certainly cause trouble at some awkward corner later on, even if it is done convincingly at the time. This is true of almost all the classical quartets and of many modern ones as well. In the first movement of the Ravel Quartet, for instance, the composer marks several decisive changes of tempo in addition to all the smaller nuances the players are expected to put in themselves. These must be held in place by a stable (though not an inflexible) tempo primo. Should that falter the movement will fail to hang together as a whole.

The firmer the basic tempo, the more scope it gives at every point. Time can be taken to turn corners and finish phrases convincingly, because there is no danger that the music will begin to sag. Every detail can be relished too, with the knowledge that it will fall within a secure and satisfying shape. There is nothing high-falutin' about it, and interpretation never comes out quite the same way twice. It is rather like the ancient, elusive search for truth, in which all four players join, playing the notes as best they may, fitting in, prompting each other and constantly adjusting their time and tone.

THE QUARTETS

Vienna: the Golden Age

HAYDN — MOZART — BEETHOVEN — SCHUBERT

FOR the best part of a century Vienna was the centre of the most glorious flowering of music the world has ever known. So far as string quartets are concerned it may be dated from 1749, when Haydn was expelled homeless from St Stephen's, to 1828, when Schubert died in that tiny airless room which was all his brother had to spare.

Momentous things were to happen in Europe during those eight decades, and conditions for musicians changed. Haydn was content to serve the Esterházy family for nearly thirty years, respectfully fulfilling the exacting duties laid down in his contract of employment and never overstepping the status of a servant vis-à-vis his master. Mozart, fêted as a child, was rebellious in a post that ranked between the valets and the cooks, and, when opportunities opened up for him at the French and German courts, could not bring himself to show the deferential flattery that contemporaries such as Dittersdorf found so rewarding. A little later, bursting upon Vienna when revolution was in the air, Beethoven rode roughshod over his patrons with magnetic arrogance. True, he still addressed his excuses to Archduke Rudolph with meticulous respect, but the excuses themselves were so frequent and flimsy, if indeed he even remembered them, that his disregard was plain to see. Schubert, later still, barely entered this aristocratic world, but found support amongst the new middle-class intelligentsia that was beginning to emerge. The nobility were poorer by that time. After the turn of the century Prince Nicholas the Magnificent could no longer have built his fabulous Hungarian Versailles at Esterháza. Musical establishments had to be curtailed and a new body of professional musicians was growing up to replace the musical servants who could no longer be employed full-time. By the time Schubert died the sedan chair had almost disappeared from the city and, symbolically enough, the more democratic omnibus had come in.

But although these changes were gradually taking place, they came more slowly in Vienna than elsewhere. The Habsburgs were astute and, though Francis II had to surrender his title of Holy Roman Emperor, retaining only that of Emperor of Austria, he succeeded in marrying his daughter to Napoleon Bonaparte. Vienna suffered less disruption than many another European city, and Metternich saw to it that neither the aristocracy nor the people had scope to concern themselves with economic or political affairs. They were encouraged to amuse themselves and, with the Habsburgs' traditional love of music setting the imperial seal on national talent, it was to music that they turned most naturally. At a time when much of Europe was preoccupied with sterner things, Vienna thus enjoyed a unique opportunity to pursue its musical interests with abandon. Its zeal may be judged by the fact that some of the performances began at six in the morning.

The inner city did not change very much during this golden age. Fear of attack by the Turks had disappeared, but a wide tactical strip of open ground was still kept clear around the city walls, a circular park, as it were, within easy reach of every citizen. Further out were the newer palaces and suburbs that could now be safely built – Count Rasoumovsky's luxurious embassy was put up beyond this ring, and Haydn bought himself a sizeable house midway between the new royal palaces of Belvedere and Schönbrunn, a house which his wife thought would suit her admirably in widowhood but which, to his relief, she did not live to enjoy. In the heat of the summer everyone who could manage it moved out – Beethoven's favourite retreats were Heiligenstadt, rising up into the Vienna Woods to the north, and Mödling to the south, on the foothills of the Alps. On public holidays, then as now, all Vienna crossed the Danube Canal to the Prater, presented to the people by Joseph II in 1766. Here they could wander through woods that still sheltered deer and wild boar, or visit the fair, hear the harpists and the barrel organs, dance to the waltzes of Johann Strauss the First and get a paper silhouette cut astonishingly quickly on the spot (the only indication that remains of the appearance of many a musician well known in his day).

During the winter season, when the nobility were in residence, musical life was centred within the comparatively narrow boundaries of the inner city. When Beethoven lodged in Count Pasqualati's smart new house on the Mölker Bastien, with its fine views to the north, as he did from time to time when his lodgings elsewhere became intolerable, he could easily walk in fifteen minutes to Bogner's Coffee House, his favourite haunt just short of the city boundary the opposite side. Passing St Stephen's en route he would have been only a stone's throw from Mozart's old lodgings behind the cathedral, where the house rules still warn tenants of the upper floors against sweeping their rubbish down into the dark little central court. In this apartment he had aroused Mozart's interest by his improvisation as a youth, and here Haydn, having just taken part in the first performance of the six wonderful quartets dedicated to himself, told Leopold Mozart that his son was the greatest composer who had ever lived. Just beyond, still only three or four minutes' walk away, was the Stadtkonvikt, in the precincts of the Old University, where Schubert got a better grounding in music than did Haydn in St Stephen's Choir years before, but not much better food.

Had Beethoven veered a little off his route, walking down Herrengasse, the gentlemen's street, instead of cutting through narrow alleyways direct to the cathedral, he would have passed the palaces of several princes on the way, Prince Kinsky's for instance, and one or two others where he was always welcome, massive square residences built semi-detached or no more than a carriage-way apart, but completely self-contained once inside the gate, the nobility occupying the ornate baroque apartments on the lower

floors, with innumerable servants and tenants accommodated higher
up. Emerging into Michaelerplatz he would have faced the Hofburg.
Not even Beethoven penetrated the imperial court, but he visited
the palace precincts often enough, to joke with his convivial quill-
cutter Baron Zmeskall, a court secretary there, and to pursue
his litigation concerning the custody of Karl. Passing the Spanish
Riding School, a couple of minutes would have found him at the
palace of Prince Lobkowitz, who, with Prince Kinsky and Archduke Rudolph, was one of his financial guarantors. Here was a
genuine friend despite their difference in rank, who remained quite
unperturbed when Beethoven on one occasion shouted angry
discourtesies through the open door. Cutting back towards St
Stephen's he might have gone through Neuer Markt, where Haydn
had once lived and given him lessons – 'The Great Mogul' his
master had indulgently nicknamed him. Arriving at Bogner's he
would have ordered his meal not more than ten minutes later than
if he had gone direct. The inner city, in fact, could be encompassed
comfortably on foot, and friends could easily meet. Informal
musical gatherings, too, were readily arranged. Michael Kelly, the
singer, described one in his *Reminiscences*, each of the performers
being a prolific writer of string quartets:

> The players were tolerable, not one of them excelled on the instru-
> ment he played; but there was a little science among them which I
> dare say will be acknowledged when I name them:

The 1st Violin	Haydn
2nd Violin	Baron Dittersdorf
V'cello	Vanhall
Tenor	Mozart.

Haydn [1732–1809]

Haydn's famous '83' actually number eighty-four. Of these, twelve
or thirteen were written before he was appointed to the Esterházy
household, fifty-seven (or fifty-six) whilst he was in the full-time
service of Prince Paul and Prince Nicholas the Magnificent (1761–
90), counting Opus 51 as seven, and fifteen after his daily routine

had been relaxed and he was employed only part-time, as it were, under Prince Anton and Prince Nicholas the Second (1790–1809). The first collected edition was published by his pupil, Ignaz Pleyel (Paris, 1802). It had the great merit of presenting the quartets chronologically and, a further advantage, with pages and quartets numbered consecutively so that the player could easily find his way about. Apart from a few errors and omissions it was unusually well done, and it is a pity that subsequent editions were not based upon it but upon the first Peters edition (Leipzig, 1815). This is certainly more accurate and complete, but the order of the quartets is radically changed. Though printed in the customary sets of three, they are bound in a sequence which must have had some reason for it then but which nowadays has all the appearance of being a random choice: Opus 17 – 9 – 50 – 77 (with 42) – 9 – 54 – 55 – 50 – 74 – 64 – 64 – 71 – 76 – 20 – 20 – 76 – 1 – 1 – 2 – 2 – 3 – 3 – 33 – 33 and 51 (with 103). To add to the difficulties there was no consecutive numbering in the text either of pages or quartets, an omission which, though corrected since, remains as a continuing source of perplexity to quite a number of players even at the present day, since some public libraries still issue these early sets of parts on loan.

A further disadvantage, which became increasingly obvious as massive wooden music stands gave place to lighter models, was the heaviness of the parts. Some publishers had already met this difficulty by issuing some of the quartets separately, but a collected edition in more manageable form was still required and Peters finally reissued their collection in four volumes. This is the edition most commonly used today and it has much to be said for it, especially for its careful editing, which some players may wish to amend here and there, but which is basically sound. Here again, however, the order of the quartets is open to question. The works now known as the 'Thirty Celebrated' comprise Vols. I and II, the first fourteen of the most popular quartets from the 1815 sequence having been put into Vol. I and the next sixteen into Vol. II. Of the quartets that still remained in the original list, the first twenty then went into Vol. III and the rest into Vol. IV. This arrangement might in itself have been no bad thing, but unfortunately Vols. III and IV are published at three times the price of Vols. I and II. With so much good stuff available at the lesser cost, players thus tend to neglect the last two volumes, which certainly contain a handful of weaker works but which also include many quartets every bit as good as most of the 'Thirty Celebrated', as well as a number that are even better for the inexperienced player to learn. When next the Haydn quartets come to be republished in collected form there will thus be a strong case for printing them chronologically, in four volumes, at an equal cost.

Roman numerals in brackets indicate the volumes of the present Peters edition in which the quartets are to be found. Arabic numerals are used, where required, to identify the movements in the separate quartets. The opinions of the music are those of the author alone and they are given merely as a preliminary guide. They should not be swallowed whole.

The pre-Esterházy quartets were written as much for orchestral as for chamber music playing, and that, quite frequently, is still the best way for elementary players to learn them. In arranging combined rehearsals of this kind (easily done at summer schools if not privately) it is advisable to remember that two players rarely play adequately in unison, however expert they may be, and that three is the minimum required to obtain a satisfactory blend of sound. Once the general shape of the music and basic points of technique have been learnt together, the players should split up, of course, into separate quartets.

Opus 1, No. 0 in E flat: omitted from the Pleyel and Peters editions; rediscovered by Marion M. Scott and published by Oxford University Press in 1931; should not be overlooked.

Opus 1, No. 1 in B flat (iv): *Wind music; adagio tedious for the under parts; spirited finale.*

Opus 1, No. 2 in E flat (iv): *Ditto.*

Opus 1, No. 3 in D (iv): *Excellent for beginners, grateful to play and has quality throughout.*

Opus 1, No. 4 in G (IV): *Adagio weak, but attractive and playable otherwise.*

Opus 1, No. 5 in B flat (IV): *Almost certainly a later work;* probably displaced Opus 1, No. 0; *all three movements good, though much doubling of viola and cello.*

Opus 1, No. 6 in C (IV): *Suitable for beginners; scoring of the adagio anticipates the famous* Serenade; *second minuet foreshadows* Witches' Minuet *of Opus 76, No. 2.*

Opus 2, No. 1 in A (IV): *Suitable for string orchestra; good throughout, especially the two minuets; adagio has engaging simplicity.*

Opus 2, No. 2 in E (IV): *Florid and lacks distinction.*

Opus 2, No. 3 in E flat (IV): *Originally for two horns and strings; very good first movement and second minuet; original tone colour in the adagio.*

Opus 2, No. 4 in F (IV): *Delightfully naïve, but has darker colour than usual in the adagio.*

Opus 2, No. 5 in D (IV): *Also for two horns originally; attractive and playable but its adagio lets it down.*

Opus 2, No. 6 in B flat (IV): *Unsuitable for beginners but has no weak movements and is in some ways the best of the set.*

The Opus 3 quartets were written when Haydn was well established at Eisenstadt (where he enjoyed the services of an outstanding first violinist and cellist, Tomasini and Weigl), their probable date of composition being about 1766. They are no longer undisguised divertimentos, although they have not yet entirely assumed the mantle of the classical string quartet. One of the two minuets has been dropped, and there is a general advance in style.

Opus 3, No. 1 in E (IV): *Poor first movement and finale; an excellent minuet and trio; the andante grazioso a perfect gem, ideal as an encore.*

Opus 3, No. 2 in C (IV): *All three movements good.*

Opus 3, No. 3 in G (II): *Famous for its* Bagpipes Minuet, *but all the other movements also good.*

Opus 3, No. 4 in B flat (IV): *Two movements only; neither worth much rehearsal.*

Opus 3, No. 5 in F (II): *The famous* Serenade *(discard bows); the other movements have less distinction but with light, bright playing the whole work sounds ingenuous and gay.*

Opus 3, No. 6 in A (IV): *Very good value except for the adagio, which is so poor that it might be replaced by a more suitable movement from some other work.*

With Opus 9 (1769) the string quartet as it is known today was set firmly on its feet, at least one work of the six showing a mastery of form and a depth of expression that is far in advance of anything Haydn had done before.

Opus 9, No. 1 in C (III): *Has some merits musically but is rather ungrateful to play; first movement frothy and the adagio monotonous.*

Opus 9, No. 2 in E flat (I): *Extraneous decoration in the first movement slows up the speed it ought to go; good minuet and finale; the adagio emerges from a low-spaced chord, like* The Sunrise.

Opus 9, No. 3 in G (III): *Needs a capable leader in first movement and largo; an engaging minuet and trio; finale excellent fun and not too difficult.*

Opus 9, No. 4 in D minor (III): *A great work.* (1) *Fine, spacious, not difficult.* (2) *On a bigger scale than most.* (3) *Less original but has grace.* (4) *Very good indeed, though the unwary may drop a stitch.*

Opus 9, No. 5 in B flat (III): *On the whole an undistinguished, if workmanlike, quartet.*

Opus 9, No. 6 in A (III): *Tails off after a first movement and minuet that, for Haydn, are no more than fair.*

Shortly before Haydn came to write his Opus 17 (1771) he had come under the influence, as had many other artists throughout Europe, of the 'back to nature' teachings of Rousseau, the Storm and Stress movement as it has frequently been called. That influence stimulated his native delight in folksong, to the undoubted advantage of one or two of these quartets, and also prompted him to explore more dramatic means of expression, not all of which progressed beyond the stage of inspired experiment.

Opus 17, No. 1 in E (III): *An admirable work.* (1) *Bright, scintillating, reasonable to play.* (2) *Angular strength contrasting well with flowing contrapuntal trio.* (3) *Lilting sadness, a little dull for viola and cello.* (4) *Vivacious, not difficult, repeats should be ignored.*

Opus 17, No. 2 in F (III): *In parts ingeniously scored but uninteresting as a whole; the finale comes off best.*

Opus 17, No. 3 in E flat (III): *Makes ample amends.* (1) *Variations, the best to date.* (2) *Haydn pokes fun by acting simple.* (3) *A beautiful, imaginative movement, harmonically bold.* (4) *Not easy but most effective.*

Opus 17, No. 4 in C minor (III): *A magnificent work showing great vehemence and mastery.* (1) *Urgent, questing.* (2) *Repose in the minuet, but the trio very tense.* (3) *Long, but ecstatic and does not drag.* (4) *Tempestuous, with angry utterances, easier than they sound.*

Opus 17, No. 5 in G (I): *Rather an anticlimax, though better known than No. 4; minuet and finale have charm and are suitable for beginners; first movement and adagio, however, need an experienced leader to bring conviction.*

Opus 17, No. 6 in D (III): *A light-hearted and attractive work throughout.* (1) *Begins with a hunting call, gay, needs steady rhythm.* (2) *Stately minuet, sparkling trio.* (3) *Smooth and serene; double stopping manageable enough.* (4) *Excellent, but goes fast.*

The Opus 20 set were written the following year, in 1772, and were nicknamed *The Sun Quartets* on the strength of the publishers' trademark, a sun which illuminated the title-page of an early edition. Storm and Stress continued to influence the composer at this time, indeed in this set he deliberately goes out of his way to avoid light rococo charm by providing more intellectual finales to three of the works. Although fugues provide an indisputable fair share of the notes, most players are not fond of them, so perhaps it is just as well that these highbrow experiments were short-lived. Fortunately there was a lighter side to Sturm und Drang, and one is willing to accept a little over-earnestness for the intoxicating gypsy music of the minuet and finale of the fourth quartet.

Opus 20, No. 1 in E flat (IV): *A poor beginning to the set, but the finale is excellent.*

Opus 20, No. 2 in C (IV): *Very fine.* (1) *Spacious, sonorous, a cellist's delight.* (2) *Foreshadows Beethoven in its dramatic changes of mood.* (3) *Follows on most imaginatively.* (4) *The fugue is an appropriate ending if the sempre sotto voce is faithfully observed.*

Opus 20, No. 3 in G minor (IV): *Well written but, with the exception of a minuet that touches tragedy, emotionally rather tame.*

Opus 20, No. 4 in D (II): *Good throughout.* (1) *Mellow, rhythmically clear, almost plays itself.* (2) *Variations, giving every player his chance.* (3) *Hungarian panache and a tripping cello solo in the trio.* (4) *Haydn at his most mischievous.*

Opus 20, No. 5 in F minor (II): *Charged with melancholy.* (1) *Tense, falls readily into shape.* (2) *The cloud shadowing the minuet lifts only partially in the trio.* (3) *Wistful, rather pastoral; the first violin should drag a little behind the beat as marked.* (4) *A sombre fugue, taken not too fast.*

Opus 20, No. 6 in A (II): *Light-hearted.* (1) *Delightful if played scherzando as marked.* (2) *Enjoyable for the violins, but dull for viola and cello.* (3) *Has ingenuous charm.* (4) *Tricky but worth working at.*

Haydn wrote no more quartets until nine years later, when he was forty-nine. He had then come towards the end of the stimulus that the orderly regime at Esterháza and his own methodical habits of work could provide and, in the absence of emotional satisfaction at home, he had obtained it elsewhere. Luigia was not a good singer and Prince Nicholas had intended to dispense with her services, but she was evidently necessary for the happiness of his kapellmeister so he kept her on. Gratitude is due to the prince for this sensible decision.

The Opus 33 quartets (1781), known as *The Russian Quartets* from their dedication to Grand Duke Paul of Russia, who had planned to visit Esterháza, were written, said the composer, 'in an entirely new manner'. One of the novelties is that they have scherzos, in name at least, in place of the customary minuet. There is also more give and take in the part-writing, more rests too, and more variety of colour. From the playing point of view the new manner is shown in the composer's greater clarity of intention and economy of means. Generally speaking the player knows more clearly what he should be doing and, fingers willing, has more chance of doing it. The greatest advances, however, are structural. Haydn has now mastered the slow movement, a problem which he did not always solve satisfactorily before and, in his first movements, he has achieved greater tension and cohesion in the development.

This point is well illustrated by the following passage from the first movement of *The Bird*, where, in a masterly fusion of the first and second subjects, there is a most dramatic glimpse of expectation, suppressed excitement and fulfilment all within the space of fourteen bars (an effect that can be ruined, it may be said, by thoughtless playing).

In the event, Grand Duke Paul had to return to Russia sooner than intended and cancel his visit to Esterháza, so Haydn travelled to Vienna with Tomasini to present the quartets to him there. They played one of them to the Grand Duchess on Christmas morning 1781. A few days later, it may safely be presumed, Haydn met Mozart for the first time and so began the friendship that was to play such an important part in the subsequent history of the string quartet.

Opus 33, No. 1 in B minor (IV): *Immediately indicates the light-hearted character of the set as a whole.* (1) *Well poised on an easy tempo.* (2) *Should be felt one in a bar.* (3) *Virtually plays itself at the right tempo; the staccato quavers not too short.* (4) *Needs very short staccato and rapid trills.*

Opus 33, No. 2 in E flat (II): The Joke. (1) *Should go no faster than unflustered semiquaver triplets will allow.* (2) *Really a minuet.* (3) *Viola and cello set the scene, masquerading as horns.* (4) *Haydn laid a bet that the ladies of the court could not restrain their talk until the end of the work – and won by false pretences.*

Opus 33, No. 3 in C (II): The Bird, *a perfect gem, cascading through-out with song.* (1) *Needs a confident opening and a real pianissimo in the development.* (2) *Dark in colour, all four instruments on their lower strings, quite slow; trio a chirruping duet.* (3) *First violin can take his time if the accompanying parts lean forward when required.* (4) *Swallows in darting flight; keep bows, for safety, on the string.*

Opus 33, No. 4 in B flat (IV): *The least satisfactory of the set, its first three movements being workmanlike but lacking heart; the finale, however, with its amusing pizzicato finish, would make a good encore.*

Opus 33, No. 5 in G (IV): *Needs plenty of practice.* (1) *Demands Mendelssohnian lightness and verve.* (2) *A violin solo, appealing but not much for viola and cello to do.* (3) *The fastest, the most puckish and the most difficult scherzo of the six. (4) Variations; rather an anti-climax; Mozart used the idea so much more successfully in the finale of his D minor, K.421.*

Opus 33, No. 6 in D (II): *Attractive and playable throughout; has no outstanding features, nor any weaknesses either; the finale variations are more substantial than those in the preceding work.*

Four years later, in 1785, the year in which Mozart dedicated his celebrated set of six to 'my dear friend Haydn' and Haydn joined the Masonic Lodge in Vienna to which the younger composer already belonged, there followed one isolated quartet which ought to be a great deal better known than it is. A terse, effective work, it gives inexperienced players an introduction to Haydn at his best without overstraining their technical resources.

Opus 42 in D minor (III): (1) *Dramatic but compact.* (2) *Excellent minuet and charming trio.* (3) *Light, attractive and straightforward.* (4) *Interesting contrapuntal features; second violin part can be played entirely in the second position.*

The six quartets of Opus 50 were written between 1784 and 1787, and were dedicated to Frederick William II of Prussia, whose enthusiasm for chamber music may have compensated to some extent for his shortcomings in other respects.

Opus 50, No. 1 in B flat (III): *Opens with two bars for solo cello which the king could certainly have played, but he would have fluffed some of the exposed passages later on; there are more manageable cello parts in the minuet and finale, which musically have more value too.*

Opus 50, No. 2 in C (III): (1) *Good, provides practice in clean ensemble.* (2) *Has charm and gives each player his share.* (3) *Plenty of imitation.* (4) *Has verve; the awkward cross-string semiquavers on the cello best played with an up-bow on the beat.*

Opus 50, No. 3 in E flat (III): *Improves as it goes on.* (1) *Rather flimsy in performance.* (2) *Variations; gives the cellist three goes at an attractive theme.* (3) *Excellent.* (4) *A delightful throw-away that disclaims all responsibility for itself in its last three pianissimo chords.*

Opus 50, No. 4 in F sharp minor (III): *One of the finest, but also one of the most difficult, of Haydn's quartets.* (1) *Has passionate urgency which is resolved only in the last few bars.* (2) *Remarkable, full of feeling, most imaginatively scored.* (3) *Immensely effective, though severe.* (4) *A fugue concludes this great work with powerful, tragic insistence.*

Opus 50, No. 5 in F (III): *Another fine work, in a different vein and much more accessible to the moderate player.* (1) *Has ingenuous gaiety.* (2) *Known as* The Dream; *the staccato triplets are quite long.* (3) *An interesting thematic link between the minuet and trio.* (4) *A little naïve, but has vitality and is not difficult.*

Opus 50, No. 6 in D (I): The Frog. *Excellent, but far from easy.* (1) *The most straightforward movement of the four.* (2) *The decorative passages must fit in unobtrusively with the rest.* (3) *The demisemis should come decisively on the beat; in the trio clean leads are needed after the rests.* (4) *One must give convincing realism to the croak heard in the opening bar and repeated with toad-like persistence from this side or that until the very end.*

Opus 51 (IV) comprises the *Seven Last Words of Our Saviour on the Cross,* which was originally written for orchestra and was later rearranged by the composer both for piano and for string quartet (the version in which it is best known today), and, later still, as a kind of oratorio. Haydn described how the work came to be written in his preface to the choral edition of 1801:

Some fifteen years ago I was asked by a Canon of Cadiz to compose some instrumental music on the Seven Words of Jesus on the Cross. It was the custom of Cadiz Cathedral to produce an oratorio every year during Lent, the effect of the performance being considerably enhanced by the following circumstances. The walls, windows and pillars of the church were hung with black cloth, only one large lamp, hanging from the centre of the roof, breaking the solemn obscurity. At midday the doors were closed and the ceremony began. After a short service the bishop ascended the pulpit, pronounced one of the Seven Words and delivered a sermon upon it. This ended he left the pulpit and knelt before the altar. This pause was filled by the music. The bishop then likewise pronounced the second Word, then the third, and so on, the orchestra entering at the end of each sermon. My composition was to be subject to these conditions and it was no easy matter to compose seven adagios to last ten minutes each, and to follow one after the other without fatiguing the listener. I found it impossible, indeed, to confine myself within the limits prescribed.

Haydn's imagination was deeply stirred by this exacting commission, as it had been by the story of the Passion more than once before, and he showed immense resource in fulfilling it. The great music that was the result cannot be fully appreciated without the devotional atmosphere of Lent or the acoustics of a church, but it should nevertheless be studied a movement at a time as mood and opportunity offer. Players who do so will be rewarded by a revelation of musical realism achieved by the simplest yet the most imaginative of means.

The next twelve quartets, written in rapid succession in 1789–90, are dedicated to Johann Tost, a violinist in the Esterháza orchestra who married money and rather fancied himself on the patron's side of the professional fence, an aspect of his character that he doubtless concealed from the shrewd kapellmeister under whom he had previously served. The *Tost Quartets*, as they are called collectively, show Haydn at the height of his power. It is a curious twist of fate that they should have perpetuated the name of so insignificant a personage.

Opus 54, No. 1 in G (1): *Fairly straightforward technically, but it was inconsiderate of Haydn to have slipped one diatonic interval into apparently chromatic runs.* (1) *Falls perfectly into shape if kept up to time.* (2) *Masterly modulations belie the first impression of ingenuous simplicity.* (3) *Has a good swing; the trio depends on the cello.* (4) *One must keep up the light incessant chatter of the accompaniment.*

Opus 54, No. 2 in C (1): *A remarkable work with unusual features in each movement.* (1) *Bold; first violin dramatic.* (2) *The first violin provides a wayward, distracted comment on a relentlessly treading motive underneath.* (3) *Rhythmically strong, but unexpected.* (4) *Famous for its scoring, which takes the cello in slow, deliberate strides from his C string right up into his thumb positions.*

Opus 54, No. 3 in E (1): *Conventional but perfect of its kind.* (1) *The notes at the right speed play themselves, two beats in the bar.* (2) *The cellist can lead into the minor imperceptibly slower.* (3) *The decorative notes come decisively on the beat.* (4) *The second violin leads off and should remember the rapids to come.*

Opus 55, No. 1 in A (III): *Difficult and does not wear well enough to withstand intensive rehearsal.* (1) *Starts well but is exposed in the development.* (2) *The tune not quite good enough to carry all the decoration.* (3) *This at least should be played, if only for the delightful musical box in the trio.* (4) *Protests too much.*

Opus 55, No. 2 in F minor (III): The Razor, *so called because a friend accepted Haydn's exasperated offer 'a quartet for a razor'. A rather unrewarding, equivocal work which seems unable to decide whether it is serious or gay. The first two movements appear in an order the reverse of what one might expect and both lose their grip as they proceed. The minuet and finale are better.*

Opus 55, No. 3 in B flat (III): *Gives immediate satisfaction.* (1) *Good value and comparatively easy.* (2) *Makes sense at the first play through.* (3) *The triplet rhythm of the final bar is the lead-in to the trio.* (4) *Most effective and quite playable.*

Opus 64, No. 1 in C (III): *Curiously weak in the company of these masterpieces.* (1) *Does not fulfil the promise of the rich low scoring of its opening bars.* (2) *Workmanlike but dull.* (3) *Almost childish.* (4) *At least has pace.*

Opus 64, No. 2 in B minor (I): *Superb and well worth all the practice it requires.* (1) *Ranges sinuously on some urgent quest; needs a leader with a zest for travel.* (2) *Glowing, transparent colour.* (3) *A scherzo, pungent at that.* (4) *Provides a better joke than* The Joke, *the two bars rest at the end leading one to expect a final chord when there is nothing after all.*

Opus 64, No. 3 in B flat (I): *Less highly charged, but exuberant and inviting. The first movement rides fast and should be bowed*

Down bows also advisable on most of the off-beat duplets in minuet and finale (points of rhythmic similarity which contribute to the general cohesion of this work).

Opus 64, No. 4 in G (I): *Technically quite easy and makes an admirable introduction to mature Haydn at his best.* (1) *Needs decisive rhythm and dynamics; the 'Sopra una corda' begins reflectively with flautando bowing.* (2) *Firm, on the string, but the leader can lift a little in the trio and make the others follow him.* (3) *Marked adagio but plods if taken slower than a leisurely two-in-a-bar; the inner parts should veil their open Gs.* (4) *Humour preferable to zeal, especially underneath.*

Opus 64, No. 5 in D (II): The Lark. *One of the best known of Haydn's quartets, but the outer movements are a good deal harder than they look.* (1) *Becomes unsteady if the tempo is even a notch or two too fast.* (2) *The very simple accompaniment requires restraint to allow the solo violin to float.* (3) *But the under parts have plenty of contrapuntal interest here.* (4) *If they still complain, the fugal section will serve them right; best to make no rallentando at the return (none is marked, though often done).*

Opus 64, No. 6 in E flat (II): The Railwayman. *Easier than it seems and by no means as mechanical as its nickname would suggest. (1) Sits comfortably on the rails. (2) Has leisurely forward motion and, in the middle section, quite a head of steam. (3) A whistle or two in the minuet but, in the trio, only the most delicate of puffs. (4) Chugs along very merrily except for those grinding octave semiquavers when it is obviously a strain to get uphill.*

Haydn could hardly have foreseen, when finishing his Opus 64, how rapidly events were soon to move. Princess Esterházy died in February of that year and, in September, Prince Nicholas followed her. Haydn was now free and before Christmas, on 15 December 1790 to be precise, he set out with Salomon for London. During the next three years he composed some of his finest symphonies but wrote no more quartets till 1793. The Opus 71 quartets thus found him steeped in the symphonic rather than in the chamber music medium and there can be little doubt that these works were conceived orchestrally. There is plenty of evidence to support that view. The use of introductions, as in the symphonies, the multi-note chords and the need for a double bass to complete the harmony in several bars (a miscalculation Haydn had not made for many years) all suggest that he had an orchestra in mind. From the player's point of view the evidence is less tangible but is discernible nonetheless. There are movements where a greater weight of tone seems to be needed than a single player can provide, however loud he plays; the first movement of Opus 71, No. 2 in D (IV) provides the most obvious example. There are also movements in which it is perplexing to find a tempo that will exactly fit, a speed that would be satisfactory enough on the orchestral strings being unsatisfactory at one point or another on the string quartet; the first movement of Opus 71, No. 1 in B flat (IV) is an example of this kind. On the other hand, some passages in all three works are beautifully written for the string quartet and could not conceivably be transcribed to any other medium; the most striking example comes from the variations of Opus 71, No. 3 in E flat (IV) where there is an unprecedented piece of most imaginative scoring which

may, indeed, have influenced Beethoven subconsciously in the
scherzo of his C sharp minor.

Either way, therefore, it is virtually impossible to present these
works adequately in performance, so the great music which they
undoubtedly contain remains comparatively little known.

Haydn quickly got back into his stride and the three quartets
that followed later that same year (1793) are free from similar
miscalculations.

Opus 74, No. 1 in C (1): *A splendid work and the most readily
presentable of the three. (1) Expansive and secure, with semiquavers
on the string, but buoyant quavers. (2) Precisely what its marking
would suggest. (3) Virile; a delightful little trio, quite Viennese.
(4) Has its difficulties but they are not forbidding; most effective as a
whole.*

Opus 74, No. 2 in F (1): *Slighter and less hard wearing, but in
moderation even greater fun. (1) Begins with heavy foot just to show
that it is country bred. (2) Opportunity for daisy chains. (3) Farm-
yard noises rudely interrupt, but there is one last bid at sentiment in the
trio. (4) High spirits, however, win the day.*

Opus 74, No. 3 in G minor (I): The Rider. *Sterner stuff musically and technically. Needs, and can outlast, considerable work. The introduction (with grace-notes on the beat) is more essential dramatically than that in any other Haydn quartet. (1) Tempo comes best from the second subject. (2) Tempo must reconcile the minim with the hemidemisemiquaver chords, which are not just a scrub. (3) Leads smoothly on from the adagio; the trio anticipates the agitation still to come. (4) Rides with urgency; the pianos even more telling than the fortes.*

Opus 76, finished in 1797, shortly after the composition of *The Creation*, is unquestionably the greatest complete set of quartets that Haydn wrote. It includes only one work that cannot be classified first-rate and even that contains one movement that has done more, perhaps, than any other in the repertory to arouse an interest in chamber music amongst those who are new to it, the earlier *Serenade* not excepted. The first two quartets are technically the most straightforward, the second being somewhat easier than the first.

Opus 76, No. 1 in G (II): (1) *The cellist sets the lyrical character, which must leave room for building up. (2) Sings throughout; the length of the staccato notes varies according to their written length. (3) A boisterous one-in-a-bar; the trio is normally taken somewhat slower. (4) Has the exhilaration of the chase; bow on the string towards the point, with down-bows on the up-beat triplets.*

Opus 76, No. 2 in D minor (II): The Fifths. (1) *Dark colour and heavy staccato, not too fast. (2) Its playful charm much enhanced by taking the accent decisively off the beat.* (3) The Witches' Minuet; *the starkness of the famous canon and the inflexible persistence of the trio give it a quite remarkable power. (4) Can be none other than a witches' ride; will lose its character if the leader is over-cautious at the pauses.*

Opus 76, No. 3 in C (II): The Emperor. *Immortalised by the variations on the Austrian Hymn, a movement that greatly appeals to children. Amply compensates for the rest of the work, which is curiously angular and unaccommodating.*

Opus 76, No. 4 in B flat (II): The Sunrise. *Pretty difficult.* (1) *One must avoid too dreamy an opening, keeping 'con spirito' in mind.* (2) *The problem here is how to sound leisurely without getting slow.* (3) *Exact interpretation of the markings is required in the trio.* (4) *The phrasing of the opening tune is elusive and may be helped by a fairly deliberate first beat in the bar.*

Opus 76, No. 5 in D (II): *Has few subtleties, but is most effective and the largo is quite unique.* (1) *One should lengthen the dot to point the rhythm.* (2) *Sometimes taken much too slow, contrary to all the indications in the score.* (3) *Reasonably safe, but there is an awkward passage for intonation in the trio.* (4) *Cello should start down-bow; second violin has a golden opportunity to impress.*

Opus 76, No. 6 in E flat (II): *Stands somewhat apart from the rest of the set and is less frequently performed but is in some ways the most adventurous and 'modern' of them all. The Fantasia is superb, whilst the finale, with its stimulating syncopated rhythms, may have had a hand in the notorious little scherzo of Beethoven's Opus 18, No. 6. Let no quartet player think the less of this work because of the problems it presents.*

Two superb works were yet to come, in 1799. The first is the quintessence of mature Haydn as he is most generally known, assured, irrepressible yet serene. The second provides a completely satisfying synthesis of late experiment and maturity, and might thus be considered his greatest string quartet.

Opus 77, No. 1 in G (I): *Rhythmically safely anchored and keeps well in shape.* (1) *Dances mischievously off-beat (down-bow), over a prancing accompaniment that should spare a thought for the sparkling triplets soon to come.* (2) *Its spaciousness seems infinite, but four beats in the bar (not eight) will keep it from wandering too far afield.*

(3) *First violin goes pretty high and then jumps down again (but not, thank heaven, a second time after the double-bar); the trio must bounce, the quavers sounding like a drum.* (4) *Exuberant, but not unduly difficult.*

Opus 77, No. 2 in F (I): (1) *Looks easier than it is, demands a vital, yet pliable sense of rhythm.* (2) *Calls for accurate time-keeping and a sense of the comic, and, in the trio, something of Schubert's genius for letting well alone.* (3) *At least one player would select this as his Haydn desert island piece.* (4) *The secret lies in the pause over the quaver rest in the initial bar, which gives it the unpredictability that is maintained with such verve until only two bars from the end.*

In 1803 Haydn wrote the two middle movements of yet another quartet, Opus 103 in B flat (IV), and added a quotation from his visiting card admitting that he felt old at last. It is a pity, on the whole, to possess this evidence of his declining powers. The real Haydn had completed his immense lifework four years earlier, full of vigour at sixty-seven, a lifework begun with divertimentos for domestic use and finished with his last complete quartet, in which the desert island movement is based upon this immortal theme, spacious, unhurried and serene, yet so vital in its rhythm that it seems timeless, a tune without an end.

Mozart [1756–1791]

Mozart's early quartets were written whilst the world still seemed to lie at his feet and they precede his mature works for string quartet by approximately ten years. Several of them make an admirable introduction to chamber music for the beginner and two or three, for all their ingenuousness, deserve a permanent place in the professional repertoire. The principal early quartets are the Italian set, K.155–160 (1772–3) and the first Vienna set K.168–173 (1773). From the player's point of view the first set is the more rewarding of the two. Here Mozart is entirely himself, feeling his own way into the possibilities of the medium with instinctive assurance and a great deal of youthful charm. In a few months he had attained a mastery that had taken Haydn, in his early quartets, as many years.

K.155 in D: *Delightful throughout*.

K.156 in G: *Easier technically, a useful teaching piece but musically less inspired*.

K. 157 in C: *Attractive throughout.*

K. 158 in F: *Unequal.*

K. 159 in B flat: *Ditto.*

K. 160 in E flat: *Surprisingly mature and well integrated; should certainly be played.*

It is a pity, in some ways, that Mozart did not continue developing on his own, but, having come to know Haydn's Opus 17 and Opus 20, he evidently tried, in his next set, to work out some of the ideas gleaned from them. Ultimately, no doubt, this was to the good, but the immediate results, hurriedly produced, were by no means an unqualified success, indeed there is not one of these six quartets that can be classified as good throughout. Most of them, however, contain one or two movements of quality.

K. 168 in F: *The andante and minuet are good.*

K. 169 in D: *Begins well, the first two movements genuinely Mozartian, but deteriorates.*

K. 170 in C: *Weak.*

K. 171 in E flat: *Has more substance, but is unconvincing as a whole.*

K. 172 in B flat: *The first two movements have vitality and charm; the last two are poor.*

K. 173 in D minor: *Unequal but the minuet is remarkably mature.*

A few years later, on 24 December 1781 to be exact, Mozart took part in a clavier-playing contest with Clementi at the Imperial Palace in Vienna. (The Emperor, unfairly favouring the home side, allowed him a good instrument to play on, whilst the visiting contestant had to make do with one that was out of tune and had three keys that stuck.) The following morning, Christmas Day, Haydn came to the palace to play his new quartets (Opus 33), the *Russian Quartets* as they are called, having travelled up to the capital with Tomasini for that purpose. There is no evidence that the two composers met during the next few days but it would seem improbable that they did not. It is quite certain, at any rate, that Mozart came across the Opus 33 quartets about this time and studied them very carefully. Between 1782 and 1785 he wrote those six wonderful quartets (the first six of the 'Ten Celebrated') that were the result, he said, of 'long and arduous labour' and which he dedicated to 'my dear friend Haydn'. If further evidence of Haydn's influence is needed, it is there in the quartets themselves. That influence goes far deeper than mere superficialities, but it is the superficialities that lend themselves most readily to quotation. Compare the C major quartets in each set, *The Bird* and *The Dissonance*. First, the opening allegros, scored for first violin, second violin and viola.

Secondly, the slow movements.

Thirdly, the ending of the finales, where both composers set second violin and viola, sandwiched between the outer parts, the nice little problem of bringing out the interest of the final bars. The scherzo and minuet of these two works have no direct connection (although the unprecedented dark colour of Haydn's scherzo must have influenced Mozart in a general way), but in the companion quartets in E flat the respective openings are these.

When Mozart imitated Haydn ten years earlier he fell short of his model considerably, but this time he left it far behind. Though

5—P.S.Q.

Haydn caught up later and drew ahead, Mozart's *Haydn* quartets are incomparably greater than Haydn's *Russian* set. And Haydn, who had genuine admiration and affection for his younger friend, was big enough to acknowledge it handsomely.

K.387 in G (1782): *Mozart never wrote a greater quartet than this.* (1) *Must sound in 4/4 as written and not in 2/4 as sometimes played.* (2) *Avoid unmarked accents on second beats; the cello very stealthy in the trio.* (3) *Unfolds with wonderful spaciousness; long, feathery bows on the semiquaver triplets and full length quaver chords.* (4) *Should certainly go fast, but Mozart himself frequently complained of excessive speed.*

K.421 in D minor (1783): *A most compact and cohesive work having striking homogeneity from beginning to end.* (1) *The triplet semi-quavers are the difficulty and need extra space at the bar before the recapitulation.* (2) *Can sound static, should always move towards the following beat.* (3) *In the trio beware of snatching the semiquavers so that they seem to come before, not on, the beat.* (4) *The rhythm will have extra point if the dotted quavers are almost double dotted.*

K.428 in E flat (1783): *Has some awkward corners for intonation but hangs together well without overmuch rehearsal.* (1) *The second violin provides a most important rhythmic propellant.* (2) *Expansive and straightforward.* (3) *Avoid staccatos where they are not marked.* (4) *All the more effective if the jokes are given time to tell.*

K.458 in B flat (1784): The Hunt, *one of the trickiest quartets in the set.* (1) *The difficulty is to keep it light and rhythmic; the editor's bowing (Peters edition) helps.* (2) *The minuet needs firm playing on the string, whilst the trio floats poised on a light accompaniment.* (3) *Very fine; the staccato notes in the first bar should be on the string at the point; the repeated semiquavers pulsed four to a bow; a veiled tone on the demisemis.* (4) *Incisive rhythm is again the secret here.*

K.464 in A (1785): *The lightest in character and the least challenging musically of the six, so requires very polished playing to bring conviction in performance. It gains, however, progressively in strength. The first two movements have little more than charm, but there is substance in the variations, and the finale acquires quite a new motive in the development which is used with cumulative effect to round off the work.*

K.465 in C (1785): The Dissonance. (1) *Begins softly and mysteriously, the cello pulsing, say, three notes to a bow and the others just creeping in; the allegro fairly deliberate, bearing in mind the awkward scales in broken thirds to come. (2) A wonderful chance for first violin and cello to lead each other; the pianissimo ostinato figure over the fingerboard. (3) Rather difficult to hold and needs to be bowed mostly on the string. (4) Full of uninhibited burlesque; the extraneous motive in E flat a delightful touch.*

K.499 in D (1786): The Hofmeister, *dedicated to Mozart's friend and publisher of that name, by way of repayment for a loan. (1) Needs a well-poised tempo to keep the triplets and the chattering quavers steady; the figure ♪.♪ | ♩ best bowed down-up. (2) The minuet straightforward but the trio tends to rush, and, since it leads back into the da capo without a break, must be taken at the same tempo. (3) Lyrical, heart-felt, needs to flow at a tempo that allows the demisemiquaver turn to sing. (4) Mozart's 6/8s are usually hard; one can only try to avoid the tendency to rush and wait hopefully for those genuine passages in 2/4.*

In the spring of 1789 Mozart, still hard pressed for money, accepted an offer to visit Berlin and try his fortune at the Prussian Court. The ensuing events well illustrate his inability to take advantage of the opportunities that came his way. Frederick William II may have been nearly as bad a king as Frederick the Great had predicted, but he was at least a capable cellist and generous with his money, as Boccherini, Haydn, Beethoven and others could testify. Dittersdorf, visiting Potsdam a few weeks after Mozart left, certainly found him so. But then he set about things prudently. He arrived with a present of six symphonies to 'refresh the memory of the king' and took pains to ingratiate himself with the principal musicians at the court. When he left he was handsomely rewarded. Mozart, on the other hand, turned up with nothing for immediate presentation to the king and fell foul of the other musicians there. He was astonishingly rude to Duport, the cellist, whatever the provocation might have been, and when the king asked his opinion of the orchestra his reply cannot have endeared him to Reichardt, the conductor. It is hardly surprising that, when commissioned to write a set of six quartets, he received only something on account. In the event, only three of them were written. Each has a cello part of considerably more than average difficulty but, generally speaking, the other parts are not as hard as those of the *Haydn* set, nor do the works themselves demand quite the same subtlety in interpretation. Though written at a time when Mozart was suffering greater personal problems they do not, on the whole, reach quite the depth of feeling experienced in the earlier works. Nevertheless, they have great felicity and charm.

K.575 in D (1789): *The most immediately rewarding of the three and, given a good cellist, presents few problems.* (1) *The accompanying crotchets must provide some 'lift'; the triplet semiquavers before the bar-line should not delay the beat; the descending staccato quavers need not be played all in one up-bow.* (2) *One must avoid the tendency, e.g. in the fifth bar, to put more emphasis on the second beat than on the first.* (3) *Nearly plays itself, but the cellist needs courage in the trio.* (4) *Has to be steady, but needs light, lively bowing to give vitality.*

K.589 in B flat (1790): *A harder cello part and does not, in general, fall so happily into shape.* (1) *A firm, swinging rhythm is needed to hold this movement together.* (2) *Beautiful but requires the warmth and freedom of an operatic ensemble.* (3) *Distinctly awkward, far from easy to fit in the semiquaver broken chords at the speed the rest of the music ought to go. (4) One of those 6/8 movements so very elusive to phrase.*

K.590 in F (1790): *To read at sight is harder still, but practice and rehearsal yield quicker results. Technically it makes much the same demands as Rasoumovsky Three, straightforward if exacting. The two works have the added similarity of slow movements which emotionally rise well above the rest.*

Mozart produced far fewer first-rate string quartets than Haydn but he wrote much more first-rate chamber music for ancillary ensembles, in which the quartet player, sooner or later, is sure to take part. The flute and the oboe quartets and the even better clarinet quintet are obvious examples. And of course there are the five string quintets. It was probably Mozart's intention to write a set of six quintets and dedicate them to the King of Prussia, but he had completed only three of them (one being a labour-saving arrangement of his wind serenade in C minor, K.338 of 1782) when financial difficulties compelled him to dispose of them summarily. Two or three years later there followed the two quintets that complete the five, supposedly commissioned by the wholesale merchant Tost, who had been a professional violinist before marrying into business.

K.406 in C minor (1787): *The arrangement of the wind serenade. Musically engaging throughout, but some of it still plays as if it were written for wind.*

K.515 in C (1787): *Ranks in stature with* The Dissonance, *with which it has some similarity. Once the superficial difficulties are mastered, e.g. the turns in the first movement, is straightforward to play. A superb opportunity for first violin and first viola in the slow movement.*

K.516 in G minor (1787): *The greatest of the quintets and some would say the greatest of Mozart's chamber works. Closely akin to the*

G minor symphony. Striking thematic relationship between the first four movements; also a link between the trio and the finale. A work to study and play time and time again.

K.593 in D (1790): *An associate of* The Hofmeister, *disinclined to plumb the depths but somewhat the wiser of the two. Needs work but is grateful and satisfying to play.*

K.614 in E flat (1791): *Has the charm of a serenade but something more besides. Solos for every player in the andante, a delightfully Viennese minuet and a Haydnesque finale.*

There is one other work that should be in every quartet party's library, partly in case one of the violinists fails to come and partly because it is one of the finest (as well as one of the most difficult) chamber works that Mozart wrote. It is the String Trio in E flat, K.563 (1788) dedicated to Mozart's fellow mason, the generous merchant Puchberg. A divertimento in six movements, it contains so much to study that there need be no hurry for the missing violinist to arrive. The adagio, in particular, is superb. Beginning in a mood of sombre gravity, it leads to outbursts of passion,

to sighs of grief,

and to flights of emotion that soar right above the doubts and the distress,

There is nothing quite like this in any of the string quartets.

Beethoven [1770–1827]

Beethoven's chamber music, like that of his master Haydn, spans his whole career and embraces much of his greatest work. His Opus 1 (1795) comprises the three piano trios dedicated to Prince Lichnowsky, in whose house he was lodging at the time; his last work of any consequence is the Quartet in F, Opus 135 (1826). The dates of his first and last symphonies, 1800 and 1823, come well within these limits. His chamber music thus provides the best means of appreciating the extraordinary development of his powers, which led him, through a unique combination of genius, character and circumstance, to reach out further into the unknown than any other creative artist one might name. And yet, although Beethoven's last quartets dwarf all others until Bartók's a century later, the germs of them can be perceived even in his earliest works. Compare the finale of the C minor piano trio, Opus 1, No. 3, with the finale of the C sharp minor string quartet, Opus 131, written thirty years afterwards. In the one, a vehement introduction leads to a mood of breathless turbulence; in the other, apocalyptic utterance precedes a most violent assault. Beethoven's masterfully changing moods are also there. On the one hand is the second subject, simple and serene, moving by step on adjacent notes; on the other, another stepwise passage, equally simple but of such utter beauty that it was quoted by Marion M. Scott as one of the few things in all music transcending temporal experience.

Sometimes there is even similarity of idiom. The fine string trio in C minor, Opus 9, No. 3 (1798), for instance, is a remarkably prophetic work, its opening theme being based upon precisely the same four-note sequence that obsessed the composer in his great B flat – A minor – C sharp minor trilogy. These and many other striking relationships help to span the great gulf that separates the later from the earlier works.

All six quartets of the Opus 18 set (1798–1800) are notoriously exacting to play, because, in comparison with the later works, which call for understanding rather than technical perfection, they have less depth with which to cushion minor blemishes in ensemble. More than one fine quartet that could convincingly reveal the C sharp minor has been tripped up by Opus 18, No. 2 in G, perhaps the most technically exacting of the six. And conversely, of course, more than one quartet able to give a faultless performance of the earlier work has been sadly wanting in its playing of later Beethoven. These first quartets were probably written in the order 3 – 1 – 2 – 5 – 6 – 4, that order being changed for publication, presumably because Beethoven considered No. 1 and No. 4 to be the best of each half-set, a verdict with which few players today would disagree.

Opus 18, No. 1 in F: (1) *A revelation at that time of what could be achieved with a single rudimentary idea; semiquavers on the string; tidy bowing for the syncopation.* (2) *Superb, the finest conception in the whole set, said to have been inspired by* Romeo and Juliet; *accompaniment just pulsed; full note values at phrase ends; avoid unnecessary bow changes in the tunes.* (3) *Staccato crotchets picked off up-bow; keep up the impetus in the trio.* (4) *Aim for the bottom of the triplet scales.*

Opus 18, No. 2 in G: The Compliment, *so nicknamed from its courtly opening bow.* (1) *Play the up-beat demisemis down-bow; a very taut rhythm in the pianissimo.* (2) *The demisemis must be 'covered' without distorting the phrasing; the allegro really fast, on the string.* (3) *The best bowing is* ♩. (4) *Cello should begin up-bow, one bow to a bar; everything possible needed in the fortissimo.*

Opus 18, No. 3 in D: (1) *Must flow, with no hesitation in quitting the tied semibreve, but a really choppy staccato.* (2) *Second violinist's delight; pianissimo quavers full length.* (3) *Mozartian, two-bar phrases.* (4) *Apt to rush; best to begin up-bow.*

Opus 18, No. 4 in C minor: *The easiest of the set to bring off at short notice and the only one in which each movement is emotionally inseparable from the rest.* (1) *The C minor impetus carries one over the difficulties.* (2) *Needs a very well poised tempo; impossible to hold the rhythm if taken even a notch or two too fast.* (3) *Minuet straightforward, but trio needs a Viennese lilt.* (4) *Plenty of bite; several bars must be written out because of very awkward turns.*

Opus 18, No. 5 in A: *The next easiest.* (1) *A really bright staccato; keep the legato moving.* (2) *Find a tempo that will carry the trio as well; second violin avoid prominent third beats in the trio.* (3) *Wonderfully serene, anticipating other stepwise melodies in this key; keep the same tempo for all the variations.* (4) *Think ahead, with bow ready on the string.*

Opus 18, No. 6 in B flat: *Much better than some people seem to think and quite prophetic.* (1) *A down-bow for the up-beat semiquaver figures in the allegro and the staccato quavers must chatter.* (2) *Beautiful; the octave passages need care with intonation.* (3) *Difficult and, even in the best circles, often runs away.* (4) *An inflexible rhythm in* La Malinconia, *with grace notes on the beat.*

With the turn of the century there began a merciless development of Beethoven's genius through affliction, and his path was turned decisively from that of performer to composer. The source of his commanding position in Vienna, 'my noblest faculty, my hearing', was steadily seeping from him. Like mighty Prometheus (the music for the ballet was written in 1800) it seemed that he would soon lie bound in humiliation and solitude. One can read now, in his own words, of his agony of mind. But Beethoven was great enough to contain and master tragedy, and one can read also of his courage and resolution, 'I will take fate by the throat; it shall not wholly overcome me.' Gradually he readjusted himself to life and, in this, his friendship with the Brunswick family helped him greatly. It was Josephine, it seems fairly certain now, who was the Immortal Beloved of the famous love-letters. These were not written until several years later, but other letters of Beethoven to Josephine, written between 1804 and 1807, have recently come to light which show how much she meant to him at this time and which speak of her having 'renewed his ties with life'. Amongst the sketches for the *Rasoumovsky Quartets* (1806) Beethoven wrote in pencil, 'Let your deafness no longer remain a secret, even in art.' The battle for mastery of himself had now been won.

This mastery is strikingly reflected in his music, especially in the scherzo of the first of these quartets. Here he wildly throws himself from one emotion to another, with savage satisfaction, so it seems, at having them at last so firmly under his command. There is waywardness from the very beginning, even perversity. And then there follow, with bewildering abruptness, moments of tenderness, outbursts of fury, spasms of pain, memories of grief and unexpected flashes of bucolic humour. Small wonder that this movement was dismissed by contemporaries as 'a patchwork by a madman' and that one famous cellist trampled on his part in scorn.

Opus 59, No. 1 in F: *Undoubtedly the greatest of the Rasoumovsky set. (1) Wonderful long lines; second violin must set the tempo decisively; a tight, dry sound in the pianissimo fugato. (2) Keep up the sempre scherzando; one must give a forward thrust to the semiquavers on the first beat of the bar. (3) One of the greatest adagios Beethoven wrote; one bow to a bar if possible; a husky sound for the sobs of grief on first violin and cello; the cadenza must be confident and convincing. (4) Beethoven changes the character of the Russian theme, making it rather ungrateful to play; one needs a clear head for this movement, with economical bowing on the string.*

Opus 59, No. 2 in E minor: *The least substantial of the three and in some ways the hardest to bring off. (1) Difficult for ensemble; needs clear leads and smooth joins. (2) Beethoven said he conceived it gazing at the stars; a heavenly movement in more senses than one and very satisfying to play. (3) The Russian theme seems rather tame once one has heard it in* Boris Godunov. *(4) Effective and not too difficult so far as notes are concerned; bracket two bows to a bar.*

Opus 59, No. 3 in C: *Needs practice but musically is mostly straightforward and is very effective in performance. (1) Rigid rhythm and careful balance in the introduction; fling oneself to the top of the scales in broken thirds. (2) Wistful and elusive, needs great subtlety of colour and rhythm. (3) Tricky, requires very smooth playing; coda ditto. (4) A most exciting fugue; on the string, fairly smooth; observe the pianos to bring out the climaxes.*

The *Harp Quartet* belongs to 1809, which, along with the piano sonata *Les Adieux* and the *Emperor Concerto*, was quite an E flat year. Musically it is the most facile of the quartets after Opus 18, indeed it may have been written partly as a duty offering to Prince Lobkowitz, one of the three guarantors of the annuity which had just been arranged in order to keep Beethoven in Vienna. Technically it is as difficult to bring off as a Mendelssohn quartet.

Opus 74 in E flat: (1) *The 'harp' movement; needs virtuoso playing and impeccable ensemble.* (2) *Pleasantly attractive and more manageable.* (3) *Should not go so fast that the incessant hammering of the cello is lost.* (4) *Agreeable if nothing more.*

The Quartet in F minor (1810) was written fourteen years before the composition of the next quartet, Opus 127 in E flat. Despite this long interval in the life of a composer whose development can be traced almost entirely through his string quartets, it stands on the very threshold of the later works. Mendelssohn thought it the most characteristic piece that Beethoven ever wrote and, curiously enough, it occupies much the same place in Beethoven's development as Mendelssohn's Quartet in F minor, written when he was two years younger, does in his. Had Beethoven died soon after its composition it would have clearly shown, like Mendelssohn's, that he had great depths of feeling still lying dormant and unreleased. Terse to the point of abruptness, it is most appropriately dedicated to Baron Zmeskall, court secretary, amateur cellist and the composer's self-appointed quill-cutter, 'His Zmeskallian Zmeskallity. Best of Music Counts, Baron Muckcartdriver' as Beethoven affectionately called him in the course of an equally terse, and ribald, correspondence extending over many years.

Opus 95 in F minor: *A most useful work to have in the repertoire; big Beethoven, yet short and easier technically than the Rasoumovskys.* (1) *Alternates rapidly between savagery and serenity; requires convincing changes of colour within the basic tempo.* (2) *Begins with other-worldly sounds not heard in Beethoven before; needs spaciousness and absolutely even notes.* (3) *Best to bracket the first beat down-bow; note that there are sometimes quavers, not semiquavers, on the up-beat; second violin should lean forward in the trio, with a light, floating bow. (4) Introduction slow and intense; the coda goes like the wind, with no crescendo till marked.*

During the long interval that elapsed between Opus 95 and Opus 127 a profound psychological conflict arose in Beethoven that brought his output almost to a standstill for several years but which also provided the driving force for him to sublimate his feelings and go on to write his greatest works. The conflict centred, of course, on his nephew Karl. Beethoven's hatred of Karl's mother and his possessiveness of his nephew, which ultimately drove the distracted young man to attempt suicide, are aspects of his character which have been shirked by his biographers. The facts, however, are an aid to understanding and need bring no disillusionment. The greatness of Beethoven remains unchallenged. His music and the nobility of its conception are still the same. His human weaknesses and miseries and tensions serve only to show, by their very intensity, why his soul was goaded into so complete a bodily release. The blind rages, the perversity and indecision, the extravagant ideas are all refined and recreated in the music. Even love and hate are strangely rarified, attaining a spiritual quality of utmost purity. It is, in fact, this complete metamorphosis of emotions experienced on a different plane that makes at least three of these last quartets, written after Beethoven had ceased composing in other forms, quite unique. Here he sees visions of another world such as are given only to the few, and to none who has not trod bitterly in darkness.

Opus 127 in E flat: *The first performance was a failure because the leader, Beethoven wrote, 'being so very stout, wants more time than formerly before he can grasp anything'. Even today is not an easy work to grasp. (1) Fine, spacious and playable. (2) Variations; beautiful but difficult; the best tip is to take time. (3) Spikey and exposed; needs short bows on the string. (4) Sounds weak if played 'carefully'; needs a good swing to carry it.*

Opus 132 in A minor (five movements), Opus 130 in B flat (six movements) and Opus 131 in C sharp minor (seven movements) were written, in that order, in 1825–26. If the Grosse Fuge (Opus 133) is replaced in its original position as the finale of the B flat quartet, these three works form a wonderful, well-integrated trilogy. They were written during the period of acute emotional disturbance that preceded Karl's attempted suicide, except that the C sharp minor was not completely finished until shortly afterwards (it is appropriately dedicated to Baron Stutterheim, who took Karl into his regiment on his recovery and to whom Beethoven was thus, as he said, 'under great obligation'). The connecting link is the 'tone-row' A – G sharp – F natural – E which appears in one guise or another in the slow introduction and first movement of the A minor, as the subject of the Grosse Fuge and in the first and last movements of the C sharp minor.

The three quartets, in their different ways, are so uniformly great that it is idle to argue which is the best of them. General opinion favours the C sharp minor. From the player's point of view, however, it is best to start with the A minor.

Opus 132 in A minor: *Technically easier than the Rasoumovskys, though calling for a more decisive, rhetorical conception of the music. (1) Very little vibrato in the opening; turn the corners decisively in the allegro and avoid bulges in the middle of the bar. (2) Depends on lilt. (3) The tempo is governed by the third appearance of the Lydian chorale; one must count 4 not 8. (4) The first beat should not sound as if it were the fourth. (5) Difficult, with a passage for the cello up in the rosin, but its impetus helps to carry it.*

Opus 130/133 in B flat: *Even without the Grosse Fuge this is the most exacting of the trilogy technically and with it is formidable in the extreme. (At least one superb performance, by the Loewenguth Quartet, suggests that the Grosse Fuge should undoubtedly go back where it originally belonged.) The first three movements make great demands upon the players, but the well-known alla danza tedesca and the celebrated cavatina are much easier technically and should be played, whilst the printed finale, although musically inferior to the rest of the work, is not as hard as the finale of Rasoumovsky One.*

Opus 131 in C sharp minor: *This quartet reveals more secrets of the universe than any other and does so, for all its seven movements, in one complete and shining revelation. If any work from the whole realm of music were to be selected as the epitome of sublimation surely it would be this. The mysticism of the opening fugue gives place to poised but unpredictable flights of fancy in the second movement. The third, declamatory at first and soaring towards the end, leads into the utter peace, in so many forms, virile yet relaxed, of movement four. The scherzo is eerie, an amazing sound for a deaf man to invent. The sixth movement shows that life cannot be lived fully without much pain and the finale that one way at least of mastering it is by unrelenting drive. Yet even here there are dazzling glimpses of heaven and, ultimately, an olympian shrug of the shoulders as Beethoven brings the whole thing to an end with three perfunctory chords.*

After Karl's discharge from hospital time was needed before he could join his regiment, so he went with Beethoven to stay with his other uncle, Johann, for a time. Here Beethoven, apparently oblivious to the damage he had already caused, was as unreasonably possessive and suspicious as before, but Karl was now detached and self-assured. He was considerate, even, to the end. 'Will you let me go for a little now? I need it only for my relaxation, I will come back later. I only want to be alone for a little now – will you let me go to my room?' he wrote in his uncle's conversation book. Beethoven's hold over his nephew, his creative driving force, had snapped. The cirrhosis of his liver got rapidly worse and it only remained to him to write two more works, the substitute finale for the B flat quartet and the Quartet in F, Opus 135 (1826). The first is a good movement by any standard except Beethoven's, but in the context of Opus 130 it is trivial. The second, it has sometimes been suggested, is a swan-song coloured by the cryptic 'The decision hard to take. Must it be? It must be!' with which Beethoven headed the finale. Documentary evidence shows this to be a quotation from a canon jokingly written some time before concerning the settling of a bill, which the composer repeated on this occasion because he could barely spur himself to complete the

work. Its presence here might thus signify anything from sardonic
humour to surrender of the spirit. The music itself is enigmatic and
might be quoted in support of either view, but, however one looks
at it, the whimsical fragmentation of the first movement, the wistful
restraint of the adagio and the inescapable reiteration of 'Must it
be?' in the finale cannot be overlooked. There could be no doubt,
even if it were an isolated work, that this is the music of a great
master. Everyone must decide for himself whether it is the music
of a visionary still penetrating the unknown or of a seer who has
withdrawn already from life's struggle.

Schubert [1797–1828]

'They greatly praise Schubert, but it is said he hides himself,'
wrote Karl in his uncle's conversation book in 1823. Beethoven and
Schubert both frequented Bogner's Coffee House, but the only
indication that they ever met comes from two self-important
contemporaries notoriously prone to improve the facts. Apparently,
to judge from a lack of better evidence, they kept to their own
circles, Beethoven a giant remote in his deafness and Schubert a
very diffident young man.

No other composer has so well portrayed the poignancy of
youth, with its impulsiveness and indecision, gaiety and languor, its
ecstasy and pain. And no other composer of chamber music is so
Viennese. Time and again one feels the infectious lilt of the café
band. There are several striking instances in the Octet (1824) and
in the *Trout* Quintet (1819); in the quartets, the most obvious
examples occur in the finale of the A minor and in the trio of the
G major. Relaxed and confident the music plays itself, and it is a
mistake to do much more than let it run. Schubert is also unique in
his portrayal of bewilderment and dread. In 'Frozen Tears', the
third song in *The Winter Journey*, there is a distracted feeling in
the rhythm that comes straight from the heart of the stumbling
traveller who cannot comprehend his grief. There is much the same
quality in the minuet of the A minor, which is rhythmically very
subtle. There is no vacillation, however, when Schubert pictures

dread, but the inflexibility of an automaton. Towards the end of his journey the traveller comes to 'The Signpost' pointing along the path from which there is no return. He gazes at it, transfixed in fascinated horror, whilst the rhythm, unrelenting as fate itself, proceeds with cruel rigidity. It is such a simple rhythm, of such deliberate monotony, but it requires the greatest concentration in performance if its fixity is to be maintained. The same is true of 'Death and the Maiden', as much in the theme of the slow movement of the D minor quartet as in the song itself. The whole of that movement, in fact, is made the tauter if this basic rhythm shadows each one of its five variations and if the tempo is set ₵ Andante con moto, not quite as slow as it is sometimes played. Emotion, indeed, is usually strongest when confined.

A little hesitation in the rhythm, in true Viennese tradition, is implied in much of Schubert's music, serious as well as gay, and, though slight, it needs to be decisive. The player should settle upon a particular beat as his rhythmic pivot and feel strongly where it is. Sometimes Schubert indicates such places after a fashion, but usually not at all. In the trio of *Death and the Maiden* he marks a ritardando and then forgets to put an 'a tempo' in. At first sight the obvious point might seem to be the return of the tune but the pivot beat is clearly the one here indicated by a pause, the tempo being immediately taken up the following bar. That, in fact, is what the editors have marked.

At the beginning of *The Satz* nothing is indicated, yet some break in the rhythm, quite small, is required if the phrasing is to be given definition. The pauses now inserted at the crucial points are obviously exaggerations but they serve some purpose, a valid test for phrasing being to submit the music to caricature and see whether it still retains its characteristic features.

6—P.S.Q.

At the end of the first movement of *Death and the Maiden* a similar hesitation is implied on a rest.

In both examples, where it is clearly necessary to round off the phrasing in some way, a momentary hesitation is preferable to a rallentando, however slight, because a hesitation does all that is required whilst maintaining at the same time greater rhythmic tension.

It might be expected that Schubert's early quartets, written for home consumption by a genius in his teens, would be ideal material with which the inexperienced amateur might begin, but the fact is that most of them are either harder than they look or do not merit the expenditure of much rehearsal time.

D.18 in C minor (1812): *Immature.*

D.36 in B flat (1812–13): *Much better; first movement rather fussy, but the others all good.*

D.46 in C (1813): *A more polished piece of craftsmanship and technically easier to play but less inspired.*

D.68 in B flat (1813): *Comprises only the first and last movements, both excellent and manageable enough.*

D.74 in D (1813): *The best of the early quartets for inexperienced players to learn; musically attractive throughout and not difficult technically but gives ample scope for sensitive ensemble playing.*

D.87 in E flat (1813): *Obvious enough to be read through by competent players at sight but not worth much rehearsal time.*

D.94 in D (1813): *Ditto.*

D.112 in B flat (1814): *Excellent all through, but unfortunately by no means easy.*

D.173 in G minor (1815): *Attractive throughout and not too difficult, but would sound just as well, probably better, on a string orchestra.*

D.353 in E (1816): *Unequal and quite exacting but has enchanting snatches of melody and some imaginative scoring most prophetic of later Schubert.*

Schubert's three great string quartets, in A minor, D minor and G major, were written between 1824 and 1826, but they were nobly heralded in 1820 by the *Quartetsatz* in C minor, D.703. Had the quartet of which it was to form the first movement ever been completed it would undoubtedly have been a superb addition to the repertoire, but, alas, only a fragment of the next movement, which promised to be a most moving andante, was ever written. (This fragment, of some forty bars, was played before one performance of *The Satz*, so that the audience should realise what they had missed, and, as it petered out, an audible sigh of disappointment and frustration escaped them.) *The Satz* itself has great variety of underlying rhythm, ranging from urgency to hesitation and from well-poised lilt to oratorical emphasis. That, together with the varied tone colour that is implied, is what brings this intensely dramatic movement to life.

Each of the remaining quartets is a masterpiece in its own quite individual way.

D.804 in A minor (1824): *The 'musikant', the so-called artless Schubert, wistfully lilting and appealing immediately to its audience. The main problem in performance is to maintain its flow and ensure that the accompanying notes do not obtrude.* (1) *Marked in 4 but should be thought in 2; the purpose of the fourth beat semiquavers is simply to propel the following first beat.* (2) *In the fourth bar the leader should lean on the first note, not the second, and take time over the final beat; the semiquavers, when they appear, need only be 'covered'.* (3) *It adds point to the rhythm to lengthen the dot in the opening figure; the first rhythmic pivot obviously occurs in the fifth, fortepiano, bar.* (4) *Requires clean, incisive playing but musically is not difficult; the grace notes are played before the beat.*

D.810 in D minor (1826): Death and the Maiden. *Contains none of the resignation of the A minor but only pleading and struggle against unyielding fate.* (1) *No third beat until the seventh bar, but vital here; the poignant opening phrase appears only once and its final pause must be most deliberately placed; the first seven bars of semiquavers played by the first violin are much better scored in the recapitulation and it is customary to rescore the passage in the exposition accordingly; the coda often flags and should maintain a taut rhythm from the tempo primo to the very end.* (2) *See page 81.* (3) *Savagely decapitated of its final note; needs a held rhythm with grace notes crunched as nearly as possible on the beat; a floating tone in the trio.* (4) *Count one in a bar and bow* down-up, down-up, down-up.

D.887 in G (1826): *Gives a vivid picture of the immense power Schubert would have attained had he lived even two or three years more; the first two movements reach far ahead even of* Death and the Maiden; *unfortunately not often played, partly because audiences prefer the Schubert that they know, and partly because it all requires masterly playing to bring off; what tunes the cellist is given to play, and what opportunities, even in mere tremolos, to lead the whole quartet!*

There remains one supreme work, which every quartet party is sure to play time and time again, given the help of a second cellist.

It is, in fact, regarded nowadays as the cellist's desert island piece, although, curiously enough, it lay unplayed for more than twenty years after the composer's death. It has certainly made up for its early neglect since then; some of its considerable influence upon subsequent composers is mentioned under Dohnányi.

D.956, Quintet in C, Opus 163 (1828): (1) *Begin up-bow; bow* ♪ | ♩. ; *announce the tune* mp *at bar 60, but drop to* pp *at bar 66; turn before the chord preceding the double bar; play the detached quavers from bar 262 on the string, with a very speedy bow; the first beat of bar 429 must tell.* (2) *Inner parts should try to keep to the bowing marked; vibrato on the pizzicato; very clear F minor syncopation, second cello don't hurry; absolutely strict time at bars 58–63; second cello merely murmurs the hemidemisemi runs and should give a long final quaver in bar 92.* (3) *Often bowed* ♩ | ♩. | ♩ ♩ ♩ | ♩ ♩ ♩ | ; *in the trio a comfortable tempo is* ♩ = ♩. *and it must be kept strict.* (4) *It is customary for the first cello to help his partner with the bottom Gs, B flats, etc.; keep the texture light; several spots where deliberate Viennese 'placing' is required.*

The Romantics

MENDELSSOHN — SCHUMANN — BRAHMS — FRANCK —
ELGAR — DOHNÁNYI

WITH the death of Schubert the golden age of quartet writing came
to an end and Vienna ceased to hold the musical initiative in Europe,
not regaining it until Brahms settled there more than thirty years
afterwards. The intervening years yielded no quartets to compare
with the greatest from Vienna, but a remarkable boy from Hamburg
was already writing chamber music that outshone anything written
by Mozart or Schubert at that age and was also, in his letters to his
sister, summing up the principal musical figures in Paris in devas-
tating terms, '. . . but remember, my dear child, that these people
do not know a single note of *Fidelio*. . . '.

Mendelssohn [1809–1847]

Mendelssohn would have been a great man had he never written a
note of music. He was an outstanding musicologist, virtuoso and
administrator all in one. He rediscovered J. S. Bach, his powers at
the keyboard were phenomenal (even on the viola he seems to have
held his own) and, as founder and first director of the Leipzig
Conservatoire, he had exceptional vision. But perhaps his most
characteristic quality was his unfailing courtesy. How delightfully he
contrived to cheer up Clara Schumann when, immersed in household
tasks, she became depressed about her playing. 'I will gladly play
the *Appassionata* if you wish,' he agreed at a musical party, 'but
only Mme. Schumann can manage the last movement, so she must
promise to play that.'

Mendelssohn's quartets dropped out of the repertoire years ago,
but there are welcome signs that they are beginning to return.
The only thing wrong with them is that they are difficult to play.
They call for first-rate fiddling, with sparkling bowing and agile
left hand, and a fluent, rather extrovert approach. Seriousness of

purpose, seeking to reveal some inner meaning, will do little good. It is sheer exuberance of playing that is required. And Mendelssohn provides ample scope for that.

Opus 12 in E flat (1829): *Effective throughout with a delightful canzonetta in Mendelssohn's best G minor fairy vein.*

Opus 13 in A (1827): *A fine adagio and scherzo but the two outer movements rather orchestral in style.*

Opus 44, No. 1 in D (1838): *The weakest of the six, but the two middle movements straightforward and comparatively easy.*

Opus 44, No. 2 in E minor (1837): *Good throughout but much more difficult; first and last movements taut and vigorous; a first-rate scherzo and a delightful 'song without words'.*

Opus 44, No. 3 in E flat (1838): *Equally difficult but less rewarding; an interesting scherzo, however.*

Opus 80 in F minor (1847): *The strongest and most dramatic of them all; the first movement has passionate urgency, there are demons not fairies in the scherzo, the adagio is full of longing and the finale seeks but does not find; had Mendelssohn reached even forty he would undoubtedly have had far more to say.*

The greatest treat of all can be enjoyed only on those rare occasions when a double quartet can be got together. What an astonishing work it is from a boy of only sixteen years! And what fun it is to play!

Opus 20, Octet in E flat (1825): *The danger is to observe too closely Mendelssohn's direction, 'This octet must be played by all instruments in symphonic orchestral style'; one can easily overdo it. (1) Tempting to play too loud and over-emphasise first beats; very taut rhythm needed in the exciting development. (2) So much variety that it can become disjointed; one must keep it con moto. (3) Fairies on May Day*

Eve, rivalled only by those on Midsummer Night the following year; a real test for light spiccato playing. (4) *Someone usually gets out before Letter A, but most exhilarating all the same; spare a thought for the leader now and then; and don't be surprised to hear the scherzo.*

Schumann [1810–1856]

Schumann dedicated his three string quartets to Mendelssohn. They were written in 1849 about eighteen months after his marriage, following a close study with his wife of the quartets of Haydn and Mozart. Clara wrote in her diary, after hearing the first of them, 'Now, for the first time, do I begin to take pleasure in chamber music, for hitherto, I must frankly confess, this kind of music has bored me.' They are not works which anyone nowadays would select to make converts for chamber music. Schumann was the first substantial composer who was not a string player, and there can be no denying he was experimenting here. Brahms experimented for twenty years before releasing his first quartet, and posterity may think it a pity that he tore up all his earlier ones. Schumann's early efforts have fortunately been preserved. They abound in miscalculations but they contain, also, so much good stuff that they give a clear and exasperating indication of all he might have done had his health not been so grievously impaired. They are still worth playing through, and playing more than once.

Opus 41, No. 1 in A minor: (1) *Starts well but degenerates into contrivance.* (2) *Effective and the intermezzo sounds well on strings.* (3) *Pianistic.* (4) *Rather thick and square.*

Opus 41, No. 2 in F: (1) *Fluent and lyrical.* (2) *Less effective; Schumann writes twelve bars of syncopated 12/8 without a single note from any player on the beat.* (3) *Good.*

Opus 41, No. 3 in A: *The best of the three.* (1) *Good use of Schumann's falling fifth.* (2) *Pure Schumann at his best.* (3) *and* (4) *are unfortunately weaker.*

The quartets were immediately followed by Schumann's best chamber work, which happily played some part in the reconciliation of Clara with her father. Wieck, who had hitherto held aloof, broke the ice two years after the wedding, writing to her: 'Your husband and I have hard heads – which must be allowed to go their own way – but we have stuff in us. Therefore he cannot be surprised if I wish to see justice done to his industry and creative power. Come to Dresden soon, and bring your husband's quintet with you.'

Piano Quintet in E flat, Opus 44 (1842): *A great work but can sound glib and requires more devoted rehearsal than any other piano quintet in the repertoire; Schumann used to stand behind Clara when she played it at home, tapping on her shoulders lest she took it faster than he liked. (1) The notes are inclined to obscure the music, so melody and phrasing must be kept specially clear. (2) A most complete and revealing reflection of the composer, his foreboding, agitation and tenderness all in one .(3) The piano in perfect contrast with the quartet; but the second trio shows the sort of thing pianists are apt to write for strings. (4) As much a tour-de-force as the finale of Mendelssohn's Octet; the main danger is careless phrasing of the second subject.*

Brahms [1833–1897]

It is intriguing to speculate what would have happened if Schumann had drowned on that day he threw himself into the Rhine, instead of being rescued to die in a mental home more than two years later. Would Brahms then have married Clara? If their love had sprung up in freedom and not under the harrowing shadow of the master whom they both adored, would it have ended normally or would Brahms still have shied away? And was it this thwarting of the most intense emotion of his life that set the pattern for him ever afterwards or did that pattern spring from something still deeper within himself? All one can say now is that his music is a glowing reflection of the little that is known of Brahms the man. There are so many tunes of Brahms that spring straight from the heart and surge forward rich in sentiment. And yet, full-blooded as they are, they have a certain drag on their rhythm, a reluctance to reach too far ahead, a characteristic that gives them great breadth and adds, at the same time, to the intensity of their yearning. This urgent withholding, exultant nostalgia, describe it as one will, tended to increase with the years, but it is to be found even in his earliest works. As he grew older Brahms became a greater and greater architect of music, but the material that he used underwent much less change. The tunes of the late clarinet works, for instance, show surprisingly little emotional advance upon the glorious themes of the early trio in B major, most of which was written before he was twenty-one.

Other things being equal, it is best to learn the three Brahms quartets in the order they were written. The first (1873) is comparatively straightforward, hangs together well and invites the kind of playing most frequently met in Brahms; the second (later the same year) is in some ways even more inviting, but contains certain problems less easy to solve; the third (1876), though delightful, is altogether lighter and might prove a rather misleading introduction to the bigger works.

Opus 51, No. 1 in C minor: (1) *Has strong rhythmic drive; rich clinging tone, broad marcato and long staccato are required.* (2) *Beautifully poised on its tempo; needs lingering, expressive playing.* (3) *A husky, urgent tone in the allegretto, a brighter tone in the trio.* (4) *The impetus and even some of the notes of the opening return.*

Opus 51, No. 2 in A minor: (1) *Lyrical and relaxed; requires a pliable, sure sense of rhythm.* (2) *Plenty of vibrato here; middle section very bold.* (3) *Difficult; needs a deliberate tempo; the first note of the triplets slightly longer than the last; the trio tricky for ensemble.* (4) *Remember 'non assai' and grip the rhythm; avoid sagging in the tranquillo; real fire in the vivace.*

Opus 67 in B flat: *Has a first movement full of peasant fun, an ingratiating andante, and variations in the finale, linking up towards the end with the opening theme of the work. The best-known feature of this quartet is the scoring of the scherzo, where all except solo viola are muted, a chance viola players do not get again until Vaughan Williams; in this tune, incidentally, both tone and rhythm pivot on the second beat, not the first.*

The greatest satisfaction comes from the bigger works. Brahms, it is generally recognised, needed more than four players to make him feel entirely at home, and it is in the quintets and sextets that his best string music is to be found. The more players, too, the easier his music is to play.

Opus 88, Quintet in F (1882): *A fine work but difficult both technically and for ensemble; the fugal finale particularly exacting.*

Opus 111, Quintet in G (1891): *Also difficult but even better music and, though it needs plenty of individual practice, somewhat the easier to perform.*

Opus 18, Sextet in B flat (1861): *Most attractive, and quite straightforward to read at sight; but give the cellist a moment or two to glance at the finale first.*

Opus 36, Sextet in G (1865): *Probably the most heart-felt of all Brahms's works for strings. 'Here,' he said, ' I have freed myself from my last love', and in the first movement he calls repeatedly A/G A(T) H/E. It is a work that combines the passionate sentiments of his youth with the architectural achievements of his maturity and is very satisfying (and not unduly difficult) to play.*

There are two other notable works which, though not exclusively for strings, are likely to involve the members of the quartet at one time or another.

Opus 34, Piano Quintet in F minor (1866): *See also note on Dohnányi. The reconstruction of the string quintet version is worth trying, the andante being especially good. (In the two-piano version the scherzo comes off best.*) *The piano quintet version, as might be expected, is unquestionably superior and carries complete conviction until the finale; this movement needs a lot of rehearsal, however, to maintain its cohesion.*

Opus 135, Clarinet Quintet in B minor (1891): *Needs a good clarinettist but for the strings is easier than the quartets. It is a warm, expansive work that holds its shape and should certainly be played whenever opportunity occurs.*

Franck [1822–1890] and Elgar [1857–1934]

César Franck's chamber music trilogy wears better, on the whole, than Elgar's. His Quartet (1890), an organ saga, is seldom heard, but his Violin Sonata (1886) is now an international monument and his Piano Quintet (1880), with its cyclic theme 'tenoro ma con passione' belying the famous picture of the ascetic in the organ loft, well deserves its place in the repertoire. No wonder Saint-Saëns was jealous. Elgar's Quartet (1918) was brought out for the centenary but has been put back in the cupboard since. This is a great pity. The slow movement, especially, is a perfect period piece, full of delicate sentiment and the whimsy of J. M. Barrie. If the whole quartet cannot be kept in circulation, then at least this movement should be preserved. It would be an even greater pity to see the Quintet (1918) disappear. This is the best of Elgar's trilogy and should rank alongside the very meagre handful of durable piano quintets that there is. Only Shostakovich has shown more restraint in his use of the piano. As with the Schumann, however, it requires devoted rehearsal fully to reveal itself.

Dohnányi [1877–1960]

Dohnányi was the last of the unashamed romantics. Untouched by impressionism or neo-classicism he continued on the broad highway of Brahms for another fifty years. He is not a major composer, but his Quartet in D flat (1907), lush though it is, is so good of its kind that it is likely to live on for many years. It has even been used for television ballet. The first movement, apart from the need for really decisive changes of tempo, is straightforward enough but the scherzo is distinctly tricky. It is best taken fairly steadily and bowed ♩ no further from the heel than is necessary to obtain a bounce; its trio, a Russian flavoured chorale that calls to mind Rimsky Korsakov's *Easter Festival Overture*, provides the clue to the tempo. The last movement is unquestionably derivative, going straight back to Schubert's C major String Quintet. Tovey has shown how this work influenced Brahms in his Piano Quintet (originally a two-cello quintet also). Schubert's use of C – D flat – C in the last seven bars of his finale is strikingly reflected in the last ten bars of Brahms's scherzo, whilst his scoring of the second subject of the first movement is copied closely by Brahms at the beginning of his slow movement. In fact, if one compares it with the recapitulation of Schubert's tune, where viola and first cello share it instead of the two cellos as in the exposition, the parallel is exact. At the risk of digression the two passages are worth quoting.

Dohnányi takes his finale from Schubert's slow movement. He does not, of course, equal or even approach it in atmosphere, but there are enough superficial similarities to show its influence un-mistakably. The key schemes are much the same and there are similarities at the end of the first section.

Schubert's second violin and viola start the middle section with agitated F minor syncopation, whilst Dohnányi's start it with an F minor scrub. The tunes that go on top are very similar in character whilst the two cello parts underneath are also much alike.

Schubert, who with Beethoven helped to start the 'romantic movement', is thus still present at its end.

The Nationalists

BORODIN — TCHAIKOVSKY — GRIEG — SMETANA —
DVOŘÁK — FAURÉ — DEBUSSY — RAVEL — SIBELIUS —
KODÁLY — TURINA — HOWELLS

EMANUEL BACH said one should always sing instrumental
melodies before putting them on the instrument. Schumann's
father-in-law, who had a great reputation as a piano teacher, would
not allow his pupils to read a note of music until they could play
simple pieces artistically by ear. The written note becomes necessary
when music reaches a certain degree of contrapuntal and harmonic
complexity, but, in earlier and simpler forms, it can induce a
squareness of mind that shuts the music out. Nobody who has
experienced the hypnotism of African drumming could conceive of
it being satisfactorily written down, still less being learnt from
musical notation. And there must be countless Bulgarians who,
accustomed as they are to a longer last beat in the note-groupings
of many of their national dances, would experience no difficulty
with this rhythm from the scherzo of Bartók Five, though it per-
plexes those who approach it only through the eye.

In music, of course, the ear came long before the eye, and, although
composers have no alternative but to write their folk-music
(genuine or invented) in conventional notation, that is only a
compromise. Their own nationals almost invariably play it better
than anyone else, because they have been steeped in the idiom. They
instinctively provide that characteristic flavour which the composer
cannot indicate adequately but which makes all the difference to

the mood. The foreigner is always at a disadvantage here and his quickest way of overcoming it is not through studying quartets. Some lower-brow gramophone records of the national folk-music will do far more good.

Borodin [1833–1887], Tchaikovsky [1840–1893]

The main trouble with the Borodin and the Tchaikovsky Quartets (1880 and 1871 respectively) is that, in part at least, they are so well known. The Nocturne has appeared in many guises and, in one of the most respectable of them, has been used to play out a late evening programme on the radio (somehow the orchestra always contrived to see the red light go off before the conductor did). The Andante Cantabile, ever since Tolstoy wept publicly when first he heard it, has cast its sentimental spell over countless audiences throughout the world, conveying a very different impression from the racy folk-song which Tchaikovsky heard sung by a carpenter outside his window. It is almost impossible to divest oneself of past memories of these two pieces, but it is at least some relief to play them in their original settings, where they shed most of their acquired vulgarities. Both are excellent movements, full of colour and convincing in effect. Though both are proven winners, Borodin's superiority as a quartet writer is clearly seen. Whereas the Andante Cantabile is little more than a violin solo with string accompaniment, the Nocturne gives everyone a share of both the tunes, and towards the end Borodin contrives a canon that is effective as well as ingenious. Much the same comparison between the two composers can be made throughout, although Tchaikovsky certainly provides more give and take in his other movements. Superficially one may obtain a better general impression of the Tchaikovsky from reading it at sight, because of its straightforward orchestral style, but subsequently it is more difficult in this quartet to obtain the clarity and lightness that one needs. In the Borodin, on the other hand, the scoring is beautifully clear and it is entirely the player's fault if there is any muddiness of sound. This is undoubtedly the better of the two works, and it has remained without serious challenge as the most characteristic quartet to have come from Russia until, perhaps, Prokoviev's Second (1941).

Grieg [1843–1907]

There are still some discerning, and by no means conservative, musicians who will confess a little shamefacedly, 'I'm afraid I rather like the Grieg.' It is undoubtedly a confession in a sense, because it cannot be said that the Quartet in G minor is good right through. Grieg, like Schumann, lacked that rhythmic logic which would enable many a movement by Beethoven or Bartók to be articulated on a monotone and still make some sort of sense. This quartet (1877–8) has insufficient logical development of phrase, so it fails on occasion to hang together. Grieg's familiar clichés, those figures rising stepwise on repeated notes and common chords without the third, become rather tiresome after a time. And in general it is a work which, though the notes themselves are not particularly difficult, is surprisingly hard to play musically, it being a frequent temptation to rush the phrasing and play in café style, the finale 'al saltarello' in particular. On the other hand it has a freshness that can still be felt today, and it clearly reflects the composer's delight in the magnificent Hardanger scenery. Written a year before César Franck began his cyclic trilogy, it is also a work of considerable originality. It was, in fact, the first quartet to be written in cyclic form, the opening theme appearing in different guises in each of the four movements. The device has become almost too familiar since, and is never an adequate substitute for a natural cohesion of phrases but, because of its unprecedented use at that time, the beginning of the theme, with its reappearance in the Romance and Intermezzo, is worth quoting here.

Smetana [1824—1884]

Although Smetana was amongst the first of the nationalists, his first quartet, Opus 116 in E minor, *From my Life*, was not written until the year before he died. It was thus preceded by the string quartets of several younger men. Despite its chronological position and autobiographical programme (which is reproduced in the preface to the miniature score) it is a fresh, youthful-sounding work which every quartet party should try. It is, indeed, one of the best possible exercises in nationalist playing, for although it is delightful when given a Bohemian tang it can sound dull if played too straight.

Dvořák [1841—1904]

About a year before Brahms died, Dvořák was seized with a sudden desire to see him. He made a special journey from Prague to Vienna for that purpose, travelling with the Bohemian Quartet, in which his son-in-law, Josef Suk, was second violin. When the two composers met, Brahms tried to persuade his protégé to move permanently to Vienna, arguing that it would be a better centre for his work, and then, sensing his reluctance and thinking that expense might be the reason, went on to say, 'Look here, you have a lot of children and I have almost nobody. If you need anything, my fortune is at your disposal.' Dvořák was deeply moved, and if anything could have persuaded him to forsake his beloved fatherland it would have been this heart-felt offer. But, as his first biographer said of him: 'He was a Czech with every breath he breathed . . . and could not cease to be a Czech just as he could not cease to be a human being or an artist'. As it was, Dvořák's passionate nationalism was never put seriously to the test, as it would have been had Bohemia been oppressed, so although it burns fiercely in his earlier works, it became gradually mellower with the years.

Opus 16 in A minor (1874): *Immature.*

Opus 34 in D minor (1877): *Somewhat unequal but intensely Czech. Has great depth of feeling, the adagio being particularly fine.*

Opus 51 in E flat (1878): *Much the best to learn first. The most typically Czech of all Dvořák's quartets, it is a glorious, youthful work and is in most ways the most manageable. (1) Unfolding slowly from spacious arpeggio figures, it breaks softly into a polka later on. (2) A characteristic dumka with a furiant in the middle, very effective and not as difficult as some. (3) A romance, full of sentiment but lightly scored. (4) A delightful skočná.*

Opus 61 in C (1881:) *Not very representative.*

Opus 80 in E (1876:) *Ditto.*

Opus 96 in F (1893): The American (*sometimes called* The Nigger). *For all its popularity by no means easy. (1) Can sound thick and square; the clue lies in the first few bars, which obviously need clarity of texture and a free, swinging rhythm; second subject rather slower than the first, taking up the tempo in the four bars before the double bar; also emphasise the return to the recapitulation and the ritardandos in the coda. (2) Tunes must float and need buoyant accompaniment, vibrato on pizzicato and fingerboard bowing by viola. (3) No accent on second beat in second bar; bow the trio* ♩ ♩ ♩ ♩ *near the point; also at the point for the triple piano. (4) The usual bowing is* ♩ ♩ ♩ ♩ | ♩ ♩ ♩ ♩; *cello takes up tempo two bars before Figure 13; to emphasise finale climax drop down and then crescendo strongly four bars before the triple forte.*

Opus 105 in A flat (1895): *A glowing mature work, purer Dvořák than* The American *and a joy to hear well played. But it is difficult, for intonation especially, Dvořák's enharmonic changes increasing the hazards of an awkward key.*

Opus 106 in G (1896): *Much the same might be said. It is also pretty difficult but is somewhat the more playable of these two fine works.*

Opus 74, Terzetto in C, (1887): *The stock standby in the absence of the cellist and should be in every library. Was written for two amateur violinists, Dvořák playing the viola part himself. Delightful music and has surprising sonority.*

Opus 97, Quintet in E flat, (1893): *Companion of* The American *and* The New World Symphony. *The scherzo, with its Iroquois Indian flavour, is excellent but there is banality in the finale.*

Opus 48, Sextet in A, (1878): *Somewhat unequal and technically more difficult than the Brahms sextets, but should be played more often than it is. Has rich sound and many a Bohemian touch.*

Opus 81, Piano Quintet in A, (1887): *Perhaps the finest and certainly the most immediately effective piano quintet in the repertoire. Given performers who can play the notes, it requires less rehearsal than any other. A great satisfaction to play, especially for cello and viola.*

Fauré [1845–1924], Debussy [1862–1918], Ravel [1879–1937]

The music of Fauré, Debussy and Ravel is not nationalist in the sense that it makes use of folk idioms but it is so characteristically French in flavour that it can be placed, for convenience, in this category.

Fauré was a fastidious connoisseur who, in his younger days, had the flair for writing music with an immediate appeal. His C minor Piano Quartet (1879) can be guaranteed to warm the coldest audience. Next, in the same year as the *Requiem*, comes the G minor Piano Quartet (1886), undoubtedly his finest chamber work. It is the only one in which he used a cyclic theme and is unique in the imagery of its slow movement, where the viola has a mysterious far-away quality which other composers have exploited since, but which none but Fauré imagined to lie in the instrument then. Finally, abandoning the piano for the first time at the very end of his life, comes the String Quartet (1924–5). For many years this has been dismissed by some chamber music players as tenuous, cerebral stuff, but those quartet players who have worked at it say that it grows on them (the best test, surely, of any work), and some music clubs, having heard it once, have asked specially for it to be played again.

Debussy's Quartet (1893) is an early work, but it made a profound impression at the time. It is still the best quartet example of the cyclic form (owing a great deal to the Grieg) and is the most straightforward of the French quartets to play. It is well worth learning if one has the time. On the whole, however, it dates a little, as most of Debussy's later music does not, so if opportunity is limited it is better to concentrate upon a longer-wearing work.

Ravel's Quartet (1902), though early too, is more mature and wears better, partly no doubt because Ravel, coming later, had learnt a good deal both from Fauré and Debussy. Debussy's influence is clearly felt in the use of running semiquavers as a background in the first movement (they need to be 'covered' rather than played note by note), in the scoring of the pizzicato and the bien chanté sections of the scherzo, in the general atmosphere of the slow movement and of the finale, and in the use of a cyclic theme (though Ravel uses it more sparingly and with greater subtlety than Debussy). Fauré's influence is less direct but shows itself throughout in Ravel's great clarity of style – there is nothing thick in this quartet as there is quite often in the Debussy. Every quartet party should learn one French work and, if there is only time for one, the Ravel would be the wisest choice. Apart from anything else it is the best possible introduction, with its need for 'atmospheric' playing, to much really modern music.

Sibelius [1865–1957]

Unison and octave playing is merciless in exposing flaws of intonation, and Sibelius's *Voces Intimae* Quartet (1909) contains more of it than almost any other in the repertoire. It is, indeed, his principal means of obtaining his well-known bleak effects. In the orchestra, where things have a convenient way of averaging out, it is not an exceptional difficulty, but in quartets it is most exacting for the players. This beautiful and evocative work, therefore, is not one upon which to embark optimistically for early performance, although apart from intonation much of it is manageable enough. The quartet comes chronologically between the third and fourth symphonies, when Sibelius was especially fascinated by the Finnish scene. Because it is so characteristic, one hopes it will escape the fate of most other isolated chamber works that have been written by composers renowned in other spheres. It is a great pity that Sibelius, who played and wrote so much chamber music as a boy, should have left only this single string quartet.

Kodály [1882–   ]

Kodály's first Quartet (1909), like many another early work, has too many notes and is not really worth the considerable practice required to learn them. His second (1918) is a very different story, being one of the best examples that there is of folk-song in chamber music, attractive both from the player's and the listener's point of view. It has the added advantage of being a short two-movement work, a most useful addition to the repertoire. Kodály's close association with Bartók in collecting folk-music did not tempt him to reach out equally far in writing for the string quartet and there is nothing in this work that is technically unfamiliar for the player. Perfect fifths (so awkward to finger) figure prominently in the melodic writing, however, and the scoring is more exposed than in most quartets, with several solos for each player, sometimes entirely unaccompanied. The playing thus needs to be well assured if it is to carry conviction in performance.

Turina [1882–1949]

There is so little Spanish chamber music in general and so very few string quartets in particular that it is surprising that Turina's Quartet in D minor (1911) is not better known. It is a most effective

work, well written for strings (as might be expected from a composer who loved playing the quartets of Beethoven and Mozart),
easy to listen to and technically not too difficult to play. It requires,
of course, a feeling for lazy Spanish rhythms, with loping movement
even in slow time and subtle changes from 2 to 3. That does not
come naturally to the average player, but it should not be an in-
superable barrier to learning this delightful work. One of its
features is the tacit tribute paid to the guitar. The cello plucks its
open strings, E, A, D, G, B and E (from bottom to top) in the
second bar and these are the notes that form the penultimate chord
of the finale.

Howells [1892–   ]

Only the wanderer
Knows England's graces
Or can anew see clear
Familiar faces.

And who loves joy as he
That dwells in shadows?
Do not forget me quite,
O Severn meadows.

Ivor Gurney had England in his very bones and could transmute
its spirit with unerring instinct into words and music. There was
something Schubertian in his alchemy, as there was in his appearance
(as Parry exclaimed on their first meeting, 'Good heavens, it *is*
Schubert!'). It was in Flanders that he wrote his *Severn Meadows*,
one of the most haunting songs ever to have sprung from England,
and it was Flanders that eventually shattered his mind. In 1922 he
went into a mental home and wrote no more until he died.

His closest friend, Herbert Howells, had as rare a talent as his
own and as sensitive a mind. As Gurney promised to excel in song,
might not Howells excel in chamber music? There was a great
upsurge of English music at that time and several other talented
composers were in the field, but, looking at his early chamber works

in retrospect, they show more originality and craftsmanship than those of any of his contemporaries. Forty years ago, in Gloucestershire, two kindred spirits promised more than had been seen for many years, and it is one of the tragedies of English music that their early works have not been followed up by many more.

Gurney and Howells were often accompanied on their country walks by a young poetess, Dorothy Dawe. It was she to whom Gurney dedicated his *Severn Meadows* and she whom Howells married. One of their favourite haunts was Chosen Hill. On the hilltop, looking across at the gently undulating line of the Malvern Hills one day, Dorothy Dawe asked how such contours would be expressed in music. Immediately Howells jotted down this tune, which appears in each of the three movements of his beautiful Piano Quartet in A minor, a work which he wrote shortly afterwards (taking less than three weeks to do so).

When the quartet was finished Howells took it along to Stanford, who read it through, grunted and made no other comment. Howells, a little crest-fallen, put the score in his case and was almost out of the room when Stanford called sharply after him, 'Go to the office, my boy, and fetch a large sheet of brown paper and some string.' Returning, he was given the score of Stanford's opera *The Travelling Companion* and told to pack it up for the post. He was to address the parcel to the Carnegie United Kingdom Trust (which had just invited British composers to submit works for publication), take it round to the post office in Exhibition Road, register it and bring back the receipt. This done, Stanford barked, 'Now go and fetch another sheet of paper and some more string.' The old man was obviously in a difficult mood. It was best to humour him, so Howells again did obediently as he was told. Stanford remained brusque as before, 'Take that quartet out of your bag, my boy, and send it off to the same place.'

Some time later, when he was back in Gloucestershire, Howells received a post card from Stanford which simply said,

Hooray! the Hen and Five Chickens

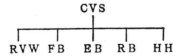

The Travelling Companion had been accepted, as had Vaughan Williams's *London Symphony*, Frank Bridge's *The Sea*, Edgar Bainton's *Before Sunrise*, Rutland Boughton's *Immortal Hour* and Herbert Howell's Piano Quartet. Altogether, between 1916 and 1928, the Trust published fifty-six works by British composers and thus made available much first-rate music which commercial publishers, at that time, might have been unwilling to accept.

Another influential patron about this time, before the days of patronage by the British Broadcasting Corporation and the Arts Council, was W. W. Cobbett, whose work for the cause of chamber music in England was matched only by that of Mrs Elizabeth Sprague Coolidge in America. It is a pity, however, that he tried to establish a new musical form through his Chamber Music Prize. Music usually needs more space to unfold itself than is provided by 'the fantasy', which has confined several promising composers to a form too narrow for their talents. Still, from the player's point of view these fantasy works will remain as a unique and absorbing store of music that is (as Roger North said of Purcell's sonatas) 'somewhat in the English vein'. A good example is Howell's *Fantasy* String Quartet (1925). It is most attractive music, full of England and not too difficult to play.

The Moderns

BRITTEN — WALTON — BARBER — HINDEMITH — SHOSTAKOVICH — BARTÓK

NOBODY can judge contemporary music adequately, partly because he is too close to see it in perspective and partly because there is much more of it than he can possibly get to know. Any review of modern quartets is inevitably biased, incomplete and of only temporary use. In judging them it is advisable, perhaps, to remember that Romberg trampled on the cello part of Rasoumovsky One in scorn and that Schuppanzigh commented, at the first and only rehearsal of *Death and the Maiden* in Schubert's lifetime, 'This is no good. You stick to your songs.' Not all modern works are likely to turn out quite as well as these, but, whatever their ultimate fate may be, patience in judging them is preferable to haste. It takes time, after all, to learn the notes. Prince Lichnowsky, a capable amateur, showed more discernment than the professionals. He patiently practised Beethoven's piano sonatas in order to show the doubters that they were not impossible to play.

Music has always got progressively harder from one generation to the next. Take the rhythm of these three openings on B flat.

Allegro

Allegretto vivace sempre scherzando

The first is the opening bar of Haydn's Opus 50, No. 1, written as a little solo for Frederick William II of Prussia to play. The second was the cause of Romberg's outburst – it made the audience titter. And the third is the opening of Bartók Five, which calls for concentration, to say the least. Peculiar new effects, too, are constantly creeping in. Haydn muted his first violin and accompanied it pizzicato in his early *Serenade*. Mozart startled everyone with his opening of *The Dissonance*. Beethoven's 'sul ponticello' in the scherzo of the C sharp minor was an amazing sound for a deaf man to invent. Schubert featured the tremolo. Dvořák brought the drum into the string quartet and Bartók the guitar. Schoenberg has gone further still. All modern music demands a new technique to be learnt and a new vocabulary to be understood, and someone has to grapple with the difficulties if a composer's work is to be heard. Bartók's first quartet had to wait two years for its first performance because no established quartet would take it on, and it was performed then only because four excellent young players had courage enough to form an ensemble especially to do it.

It is a common complaint that new music is nowadays so difficult that it is beyond the reach of the ordinary amateur. There is certainly truth in this. Obviously it is the professionals who must give difficult modern music its first hearing if it is to be fairly judged, and public patronage, in recent years, has made it increasingly worth their while to undertake the long and exacting preparation that may be required. Amateurs, however, and particularly those who have been trained as professionals but have been emancipated from bread-and-butter playing, have always taken a prominent part in supporting the contemporary composer, and there is still a great deal that they can do. Many of them know the classical repertoire inside out (much better than some professionals) and can discuss it with the discernment that comes from actual experience. Because of this inside knowledge they make the most critical and, at the same time, the most sympathetic and appreciative audience that there is. Their judgement and encouragement are equally necessary in performances of modern music, and their opinions are the more valuable if they are based upon some practical experience of what it takes to make the music speak. Nobody would expect them to plunge headlong into ultra-modern works, but it can be instructive to work at an odd movement here and there in order to get a first-hand idea of what Schoenberg, Berg, Webern and more recent recruits to the avant-garde are about. The first of Stravinsky's Three Pieces and one or two of Webern's Five Pieces for String Quartet would make a good beginning. These works were not written for the amateur, but Hindemith catered specifically for him in No. 3 of his *Schulwerk* (1927), comprising eight pieces for string quartet, and at least one London publisher has commissioned several short quartets in a modern idiom which do not stretch technical resources to the limit. There is, in fact, plenty of modern music within his range, can he but find it.

Sometimes, of course, it may be only one or two movements of a larger work, but that is no reason why the work should be discarded as a whole. Sometimes, on the other hand, it may be a complete quartet. For instance, there is Herbert Murrill's delightful Quartet in A minor (1940), a work performed with great success by an amateur quartet party who brought it with them to a summer school. It has to be admitted, however, that such music is not readily found. Comparatively few public libraries stock the parts of any quartets written since the First World War, thus lagging far behind their enterprise in other directions, and only the go-ahead player who will search the catalogues and dip into his pocket is likely to find anything interesting and playable off the beaten track.

Britten ⌈1913–   ⌉ and Walton ⌈1902–   ⌉

Britten's second quartet (1945) is the better of the two and is also the more playable. It was written in commemoration of the 250th anniversary of Purcell's death and concludes, appropriately, with a chaconne. The first movement is exposed here and there, but has no extremes of pitch or rhythm. The scherzo has some tricky cross-string pizzicato and the first violin goes rather high, but it is not impossible. The Chacony comprises its theme and twenty-one variations. These are divided into three groups of six, each group being followed by a cadenza for cello, viola and violin respectively, with three variations as a coda. The cadenzas are difficult but most of the variations are manageable enough. The first group, comprising varied harmonisations, is straightforward; the second, with rhythmical variations, is harder; the third, in which the theme is used as an accompaniment to a melody which is itself varied, is again quite playable, and so is the coda.

Walton's Quartet in A minor (1947) is a first-rate work, English in flavour and thoroughly typical of his style. The published score is a facsimile of his manuscript, a model of penmanship which it would be hard to beat. Technically it is difficult, but contains nothing which might cause competent and experienced players to despair. Most of the thematic material is introduced by the viola, an instrument that Walton has often treated generously elsewhere. The viola is given the long, singing opening tune and later on, when the same notes form the subject of a fugue, it announces this also, incisively this time. It has most of the melodic interest, too, in the lento, an expansive, lyrical movement full of the serenity of the English countryside. There are fairer shares for all in the other two movements, where the interest is rhythmic rather than melodic. The scherzo bristles with Walton's barbed wit, whilst the finale, for all its unexpected changes of time, has tremendous drive. The notes of these two movements are not in themselves particularly hard but the players need to be very wide awake if they are not to get left behind at speed.

Barber [1910–   ]

Samuel Barber's Quartet in B minor, Opus 11 (1939), is a most useful addition to the repertoire. A short two-movement work, it is not too modern to be taken in by an audience at first hearing, and it contains the famous *Adagio for Strings* (which was arranged for string orchestra at Toscanini's suggestion) in its original setting. The adagio, of course, can be played separately, although it actually forms the first part of the second movement, which concludes with a virtual recapitulation of the exposition of the first movement. The first movement itself is full of engaging ideas but judgement is needed to negotiate some of the joins.

Another useful and attractive work, to add to the slender repertoire of chamber music with voice, is Barber's *Dover Beach* (to words of Matthew Arnold) for baritone and string quartet.

Hindemith [1895–1963]

Hindemith wrote something for almost all instruments and for innumerable combinations of them and, as might be expected of an experienced quartet player (he was the viola in the Amar Quartet for several years), it is all eminently playable. No other contemporary composer has done so much to provide singers and players with accessible music in a modern idiom. His six string quartets, spanning an interval of more than a quarter of a century, cannot be said to be easy, but they are mostly robust and playable and they call for little of that wispy, atmospheric playing which makes some modern music so difficult to bring off convincingly.

The First Quartet in F minor, Opus 10 (1919), is unashamedly derivative, harking back to the opulent old days and imposing no inhibitions on the player. For those who are reluctant to forsake the nineteenth century this is a work to try. The Second Quartet in C, Opus 16 (1922), though written only three years later, has greater pungency altogether. Its first movement, strong and straightforward, is more virile; the ghostly slow movement, still with a trace of Wagner in it, maintains its imaginative interest at considerable length; the finale, an early example of Hindemith's 'engine music' as it has sometimes been called, is full of boisterous, bucolic fun, which those who are not deterred by speedy open fifths can thoroughly enjoy. In the Third Quartet, Opus 22 (1922), written very soon afterwards, Hindemith abandoned the conventional time signatures (key signatures, too), together with the last traces of chromatic harmony. This does not in itself add much to the practical difficulties, but on other grounds, notably the amount of confident solo playing that is required, the work demands very capable players. The Fourth Quartet, Opus 32 (1924), is technically much the most exacting of the six; beginning with a double fugue and ending with a passacaglia, it is more an example of professional skill than a piece for the ordinary player to use. Almost twenty years elapsed before the next quartet, No. 5 in E flat (1943), written soon after Hindemith became Head of the Music Department at Yale University. He had then acquired much more simplicity of style, and this is probably the best known of his quartets, as well as being the most rewarding to play. The texture is now clearer than before, counterpoint is used expressively as well as ingeniously and the harmony has spice without sounding forced or overdone. The notes, too, are if anything easier than in the earlier works. Of the four movements the first is quietly contrapuntal, the second very energetic; the theme and variations, unlike those of the First Quartet, are more than effective contrasts and build on each other to form a satisfying shape; the finale is the hardest movement technically but is carried by its energy and breadth. The Sixth Quartet (1943), in which the interval of the falling fourth is a melodic feature of each movement, is also clear and approachable but it calls for lighter, more fanciful playing than is needed in the earlier quartets. The first movement is straightforward enough and so is the third; both the scherzo and the concluding canon, however, often leave the players uncomfortably isolated.

Shostakovich [1906–   ]

Shostakovich has an immense musical talent which can justifiably be compared with that of Brahms. Brahms, who had been playing the piano in a dance hall, established himself as a pianist and composer when he was twenty years of age. Shostakovich, who had been playing miserably in a cinema, was only nineteen when he did the same. Like Brahms, too, he has not advanced very far beyond the astonishing accomplishment of his early works. Nobody can tell, with men of such reserve, whether this halting of their development is inborn or whether it springs from external circumstance. In the case of Shostakovich it may have been due to conflict between artistic freedom and political expediency. All that is definitely known is that at least twice in his career he has been sharply rebuked officially for the kind of music he was writing at the time.

As it is, Shostakovich's chamber music is straightforward, easy to listen to and, as modern music goes, not difficult to play. It is unmistakably Russian in flavour yet curiously, rather sadly detached, as though, Petroushka-like, it is a puppet who is expressing the feelings revealed in the notes. There is an air, too, of resignation, even inconsequence, about many of the endings to the chamber works, which float pianissimo away into nothingness – like the final curtain of *Boris Godounov*, where, after all those momentous happenings, a solitary peasant is left huddled beneath the gently falling snow. Shostakovich's scoring is always beautifully clear and, although he has not in other respects introduced anything new to the string quartet, he has made more effective use of spacing than any other composer before him. Unfortunately, from the player's point of view, this often takes the parts extremely high, but they usually ascend by easy stages and, once there, the notes lie reasonably well underneath the hand.

The First Quartet in C, Opus 49 (1938) is not one of the best. It is, however, quite playable. Apart from a highish passage here and there the notes are comparatively easy, and effective performance depends not so much upon left-hand technique as upon a whimsical sense of rhythm. Quartet No. 2 in A, Opus 69 (1944), is hardly a string quartet in the usual sense of the term, and in parts requires concerto playing to bring off. The Third Quartet, Opus 73 (1946), makes more orthodox use of the medium and musically it rivals the popular Piano Quintet, composed six years before. Unlike that work, however, it begins lightly and grows in emotional intensity as it proceeds. The Fourth Quartet, Opus 83 (1949), is altogether lighter in character and is considerably easier to play. It has charm without great depth. The Fifth Quartet, Opus 92 (1951), a haunting work, contains not a single fast passage from beginning to end and no particular difficulty apart from altitude and some double stopping. The Sixth Quartet, Opus 101 (1956), follows much the same pattern as No. 4, pulling gently on familiar heart strings and venturing no further afield. Amateurs could tackle much if not all of the last two quartets, which are thoroughly representative of Shostakovich in his more serious as well as in his lighter moods and which both contain admirable examples of his habit of transforming a theme by the simple expedient of altering the basic beat. The Seventh Quartet, Opus 108 (1960), is reminiscent of the ballet. The Eighth, Opus 110 (1960), is an altogether deeper work, convincingly designed and using counterpoint with great emotional effect. Both works, characteristically, end pianissimo.

Bartók [1881–1945]

Of all modern quartets it can only be said with certainty that those of Bartók will survive. Some critics have called them the natural successors to Beethoven's and, although that claim was also made for those of Brahms, it can now be seen to be truer of Bartók still. Much has already been written about these quartets both in England and America, alternative recordings of them are available and they are regularly heard in the concert room, often in company with Beethoven. It is thus unnecessary to describe them all in detail here. It may be mentioned, however, that they are all formidably difficult and that, if playing them is contemplated, it is wisest to start with Bartók Two, which is the most straightforward of the six. At first even this may seem distinctly strange, but gradually, as the idiom becomes more familiar, it will be found that the music calls for exactly the same sense of spacing and of emphasis as any other.

It has sometimes been suggested that some at least of these quartets are 'too contrived'. They certainly contain a great many examples of academic skill, they have a well-planned, almost streamlined shape and they tend to germinate from some quite small idea. Bartók Five, for instance (from which the remaining illustrations will be taken), is shaped somewhat like an arch. At the apex is the trio, flanked by the scherzo and its repetition. On either side are the two slow movements, different in material yet alike in character and shape, a semicircular shape at that. And, at the base, stand the two main movements, the allegro and the presto. These, too, have similarities. Both contain a good deal of canon and other contrapuntal devices, the order of themes is reversed in the recapitulation of both movements (this making another semicircle) and, in each, the first subject makes great play upon the tritone, in the first movement from B flat up to E and in the last from E down to B flat. Thus there is an over-all, arch-like shape in which movements II and IV, and movements I and V are of a kind and in which each of the five movements is itself shaped in a smaller arch. It is a singularly tidy piece of work. Bartók, of course, had a meticulously well-ordered mind and his best-known book, *Hungarian Folk Music*, if taken by itself, suggests that he had little else besides. And yet he is the man who nearly wrecked the first performance of his Concerto for Two Pianos with the New York Philharmonic Orchestra because a wrong note from the timpanist set him off extemporising on his own, leaving the other performers completely in the dark. So much for the ingenious manufacturer. This quartet, too, was written in only a month, a fact which suggests an extraordinarily powerful creative urge, and almost every accusation of contrivance which can be levelled against it can be levelled also at Beethoven.

Bartók and Beethoven have the same masterly design and the

same organic growth. There is the same polyphonic freedom and
the same daring invention of new sounds. Perhaps the similarities
might be taken further still. There are the obvious ones such as
their love of nature and their powerful piano playing, their with-
drawal within themselves and the vehemence of their attitude to
life. Less obvious are the things they have to say. And yet compare
the last movement of the C sharp minor with the finale of Bartók
Five. Is not the feeling of the opening bars very much alike – those
violent ejaculations heralding that fierce assault? Beethoven starts:

and Bartók:

More than one listener, too, though possessing little musical
knowledge, has commented upon the similarity between the
scherzo of Beethoven's F Minor Quartet and the first movement of
Bartók Five. And is not that enigmatic shrug of the shoulders with
which the C sharp minor ends matched by the curiously trite
'allegretto con indifferenza' towards the end of Bartok's finale?
In their apocalyptic utterance, their immense vitality and their
olympian detachment the two composers are very much alike, but
Bartók, although he underwent much suffering, never escaped
from the bondage of himself and captured that wonderful serenity
which Beethoven, in his music, finally attained. One feels, however,
that he was searching for it passionately. His mind went back so

often to those deeply satisfying song-collecting days in the out-lying villages, where, identified with the people, he had absorbed their simple way of life. He could vividly remember the routine of their homely tasks, the village sights and sounds and smells, and the calm that lay beneath it all. Yet it remained a memory. The sense of peace, however he sought it afterwards, did not stay with him for long. It appeared occasionally and then eluded him. And is not that elusiveness to be found also in his music? The adagio molto of this quartet begins with wisps of sound which gradually gain substance until they reach conviction in the cool repose of modal harmony, with a contemplative comment from the first violin, off-note like a wavering peasant flute heard distantly at night.

Beethoven would have retained this mood and expanded it, but Bartók let it slip. Not until some ten bars later does he recapture it and even then but insecurely. The music gradually evaporates until there remain only thin vaporous trails, the last disappearing traces of a phantom peace.

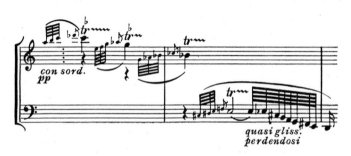

But, however elusive this may seem at first to play or hear, there can be no doubt that it is genuine. Bartók may not have found all that he was searching for but, in speech and music, he would have scorned to say anything he did not feel. Ditta, his wife, put it with such simplicity. 'All you have to know about Béla,' she said, 'is that he loves everything that's real.'

And is that not all – or very nearly all – one needs to know about a string quartet? Is it real? Does it say something that is genuinely felt?

Timings

ALL the quartets mentioned in the text, together with a few other works, are listed below. The list is fairly complete as far as the current repertoire goes, but a great many unfamiliar modern works, as well as a much greater number of now forgotten quartets, have had to be omitted. Timings (in minutes), taken from broadcast or public performances, have been added in nearly every case; where they have not been included it might be useful for players to fill in the gaps as opportunity offers. Variations in timing are mainly accounted for by repeats, but there are differences, of course, in tempo also. It will be noticed that composers' estimates, when given, are not always realised in performance.

ARRIAGA
(1806–1825)

Quartets
No. 1 in D minor:
No. 2 in A: $21\frac{1}{4}$
No. 3 in E flat: $23\frac{1}{2}$

BARBER
(1910–   )

Quartet in B minor, Opus 11:   *14*
Dover Beach for Medium Voice and String Quartet: $6\frac{1}{2}$

BARTÓK
(1881–1945)

Quartets		
No. 1, Opus 7 (1908): $29\frac{3}{4}$–33	No. 3 (1929):	15–$16\frac{3}{4}$
No. 2, Opus 17 (1915–17):	No. 4 (1928):	$26\frac{3}{4}$–30
	No. 5 (1934):	31–$32\frac{1}{4}$
28–$32\frac{1}{4}$	No. 6 (1941):	27–31

BAX
(1883–1953)

Quintet for Harp and Strings: $13\frac{3}{4}$–15
Quintet for Oboe and Strings: $15\frac{3}{4}$–$18\frac{1}{4}$

BLISS
(1891–   )

Quintet for Oboe and Strings: $20\frac{1}{2}$–24
Quintet for Clarinet and Strings: 26–$29\frac{1}{2}$

BEETHOVEN
(1770–1827)

Quartets

Opus 18, No. 1 in F:	25–$26\frac{3}{4}$
No. 2 in G:	21–24
No. 3 in D:	$22\frac{1}{2}$–25
No. 4 in C minor:	19–24
No. 5 in A:	23–28
No. 6 in B flat:	$23\frac{3}{4}$–$27\frac{1}{4}$
Opus 59, No. 1 in F:	36–40
No. 2 in E minor:	29–38
No. 3 in C:	$30\frac{1}{4}$–32
Opus 74 in E flat:	31–$34\frac{1}{2}$
Opus 95 in F minor:	$20\frac{1}{2}$–24
Opus 127 in E flat:	32–36
Opus 130 in B flat:	$43\frac{3}{4}$–45

Opus 131 in C sharp minor:
39–45
Opus 132 in A minor: 43–47
Opus 133 (*Grosse Fuge*): 15
Opus 135 in F: $21\frac{3}{4}$–23
String Trios
Opus 3 in E flat: $38\frac{1}{4}$
Opus 8 in D (Serenade): $18\frac{1}{2}$
Opus 9, No. 1 in G: 23–$24\frac{1}{4}$
No. 2 in D: $20\frac{3}{4}$–22
No. 3 in C minor: $20\frac{1}{2}$–22
Septet in E flat, Opus 20
(1 – 1 – 1 – Db – Cl – Hn –
Bn) 39

BORODIN
(1833–1887)

Quartet No. 2 in D: $25\frac{1}{2}$–$28\frac{1}{2}$

BRAHMS
(1833–1897)

Quartets
Opus 51, No. 1 in C minor:
$27\frac{3}{4}$–33
No. 2 in A: 30–32
Opus 67 in B flat: $32\frac{1}{2}$–$35\frac{3}{4}$
String Quintets (2 – 2 – 1)
Opus 88 in F: $22\frac{1}{2}$–$27\frac{1}{2}$
Opus 111 in G: 24–29
String Sextets (2 – 2 – 2)
Opus 18 in B flat: $29\frac{1}{2}$–38

Opus 36 in G: 34–$41\frac{1}{2}$
Clarinet Quintet in B minor,
Opus 115: $33\frac{1}{2}$–38
Piano Quintet in F minor,
Opus 34: 35–$43\frac{1}{4}$
Piano Quartets
Opus 25 in G minor: $35\frac{1}{2}$–$42\frac{1}{2}$
Opus 26 in A: 43–$46\frac{1}{2}$
Opus 60 in C minor: 27–$33\frac{3}{4}$

BRITTEN

(1913–   )

Quartet No. 2 in C, Opus 36: $25\frac{1}{2}$–*36*

BRUCKNER

(1824–1896)

String Quintet in F (2 – 2 – 1): $33\frac{1}{2}$–$39\frac{1}{2}$

DEBUSSY

(1862–1918)

Quartet in G minor: 25–$27\frac{1}{4}$

DELIUS

(1862–1934)

Quartet (1916): $26\frac{3}{4}$

DITTERSDORF

(1739–1799)

Quartets		No. 4 in C:	
No. 1 in D:	10–$11\frac{3}{4}$	No. 5 in E flat (with	
No. 2 in B flat:		andante added):	$15\frac{1}{4}$–17
No. 3 in G:	12	No. 6 in A:	$13\frac{1}{2}$–$16\frac{3}{4}$

DOHNÁNYI

(1877–1960)

Quartet in D flat, Opus 15: $25\frac{3}{4}$–28

String Trio (*Serenade*) in C, Opus 10: $21\frac{3}{4}$

DVOŘÁK

(1841–1904)

Quartets		*String Quintets*	
Opus 16 in A minor:		Opus 77 in G (2–1–1–Db) 32–$33\frac{1}{4}$	
Opus 34 in D minor:	$28\frac{3}{4}$–30	Opus 97 in E flat (2–2–1) 27–31	
Opus 51 in E flat:	$30\frac{1}{2}$–33	*String Sextet* (2–2–2)	
Opus 61 in C:	$35\frac{1}{4}$	Opus 48 in A:	$29\frac{3}{4}$–31
Opus 80 in E:	25–29	*Terzetto* (2 – 1)	
Opus 96 in F:	$22\frac{1}{2}$–$26\frac{1}{4}$	Opus 74 in C:	$18\frac{1}{2}$–$22\frac{1}{2}$
Opus 105 in A flat:	32–34	*Piano Quintet*	
Opus 106 in G:	35–40	Opus 81 in A:	$29\frac{3}{4}$–39

ELGAR
(1857–1934)

String Quartet, Opus 83 in E minor: $25\frac{1}{2}$–28
Piano Quintet, Opus 84 in A minor: 35–38

FAURÉ
(1845–1924)

String Quartet, Opus 121:   23–25
Piano Quartet, Opus 15 in C minor: $32\frac{3}{4}$–$34\frac{1}{2}$
Piano Quartet, Opus 45 in G minor: $34\frac{1}{2}$–38

FRANCK
(1822–1890)

Quartet in D: 44–$55\frac{1}{2}$
Piano Quintet in F minor: 35–$37\frac{1}{2}$

GRIEG
(1843–1907)

Quartet in G minor, Opus 27: 31–35

GURNEY
(1890–1937)

Song Cycle, *Ludlow and Teme* (Tenor – 2 – 1 – 1 – Piano): 18–$20\frac{1}{2}$

HARRIS
(1898–   )

Quintet for Flute and Strings, *Four Minutes Twenty Seconds*: See title

HAYDN
(1732–1809)

Quartets

Opus 1, No. 0 in E flat:		Opus 2, No. 1 in A:	$18\frac{1}{2}$
Opus 1, No. 1 in B flat:	$16\frac{1}{2}$–18	No. 2 in E:	$17\frac{1}{4}$–$18\frac{1}{2}$
No. 2 in E flat:	$17\frac{1}{2}$	No. 3 in E flat:	$15\frac{1}{2}$
No. 3 in D:	16	No. 4 in F:	19
No. 4 in G:	16–$18\frac{3}{4}$	No. 5 in D:	12–18
No. 5 in B flat:		No. 6 in B flat:	
No. 6 in C:	15		

8*

Quartets

Opus 3, No. 1 in E: $11\frac{1}{2}$
    No. 2 in C:
    No. 3 in G: $13\frac{1}{4}$–$14\frac{3}{4}$
    No. 4 in B flat:
    No. 5 in F: 12–$17\frac{1}{2}$
    No. 6 in A:
Opus 9, No. 1 in C: 14
    No. 2 in E flat: 15
    No. 3 in G: 15
    No. 4 in D minor: 15–20
    No. 5 in B flat: $17\frac{3}{4}$–18
    No. 6 in A: $13\frac{3}{4}$
Opus 17, No. 1 in E: $19\frac{3}{4}$
    No. 2 in F:
    No. 3 in E flat:
    No. 4 in C minor:
    No. 5 in G:
    No. 6 in D:
Opus 20, No. 1 in E flat: 12–15
    No. 2 in C: $19\frac{1}{2}$–$20\frac{1}{4}$
    No. 3 in G minor:
    No. 4 in D: 20–24
    No. 5 in F minor: $18\frac{3}{4}$–$22\frac{3}{4}$
    No. 6 in A: 17–$17\frac{1}{2}$
Opus 33, No. 1 in B minor: $19\frac{3}{4}$
    No. 2 in E flat: 20
    No. 3 in C: $16\frac{1}{4}$–$18\frac{1}{2}$
    No. 4 in B flat: 15
    No. 5 in G: $16\frac{3}{4}$
    No. 6 in D: 15–$15\frac{3}{4}$
Opus 42 in D minor: $14\frac{1}{2}$
Opus 50, No. 1 in B flat: $18\frac{1}{2}$–22
    No. 2 in C: $19\frac{3}{4}$
    No. 3 in E flat:

    No. 4 in F sharp minor:
    No. 5 in F: $15\frac{3}{4}$–$16\frac{1}{2}$
    No. 6 in D: $20\frac{1}{4}$
Opus 51, *Seven Last Words*:
Opus 54, No. 1 in G: $17\frac{1}{2}$–21
    No. 2 in C: $18\frac{1}{2}$–$21\frac{1}{2}$
    No. 3 in E: $18\frac{1}{2}$
Opus 55, No. 1 in A: 16
    No. 2 in F minor:
    No. 3 in B flat:
Opus 64, No. 1 in C: $13\frac{3}{4}$
    No. 2 in B minor: $18\frac{3}{4}$
    No. 3 in B flat: 20
    No. 4 in G: $15\frac{1}{2}$
    No. 5 in D: 16–$21\frac{1}{2}$
    No. 6 in E flat: $16\frac{1}{2}$–$17\frac{1}{2}$
Opus 71, No. 1 in B flat:
    No. 2 in D: $18\frac{3}{4}$
    No. 3 in E flat: $23\frac{3}{4}$
Opus 74, No. 1 in C: 19
    No. 2 in F: $22\frac{1}{4}$
    No. 3 in G minor: $16\frac{1}{2}$–22
Opus 76, No. 1 in G: $18\frac{1}{4}$–$20\frac{1}{2}$
    No. 2 in D minor: $17\frac{1}{2}$–$20\frac{1}{2}$
    No. 3 in C: 22–$26\frac{1}{2}$
    No. 4 in B flat: $20\frac{1}{2}$–$22\frac{1}{2}$
    No. 5 in D: 19–$20\frac{1}{2}$
    No. 6 in E flat: $20\frac{1}{2}$–$23\frac{1}{2}$
Opus 77, No. 1 in G: $18\frac{1}{2}$–$23\frac{3}{4}$
    No. 2 in F: $22\frac{1}{2}$–24
Opus 103 in B flat: $9\frac{3}{4}$–$10\frac{1}{4}$

HINDEMITH
(1895–1963)

Quartets

No. 1 in F minor, Opus 10:	33	No. 4, Opus 32:	
No. 2 in C minor, Opus 16:		No. 5 in E flat (1943):	25
No. 3, Opus 22:	24	No. 6 (1945):	

HOWELLS
(1892–   )

Fantasy String Quartet, Opus 25:   *12–15*
Piano Quartet in A minor, Opus 21: *27–28*

KODÁLY
(1882–   )

Quartet No. 2, Opus 10: *16–18¼*

MATTHEW LOCKE
(1630–1677)

Quartets (arr. Mangeot and		No. 3 in F:	7¾
Warlock)		No. 4 in F:	9
No. 1 in D minor:	6½	No. 5 in G minor:	8¼–10¼
No. 2 in D:		No. 6 in G:	7

MENDELSSOHN
(1809–1847)

Quartets

Opus 12 in E flat:	22½–26		
Opus 13 in A minor:	30½–31½	No. 3 in E flat:	36–37
Opus 41, No. 1 in D:	23¾–27¾	Opus 80 in F minor:	26½
No. 2 in E minor:	23½–27	*Octet* in E flat, Opus 20	
		(4 – 2 – 2)	27¾–31

MOZART
(1756–1791)

Quartets

K. 155 in D:		K. 589 in B flat:	$21\frac{3}{4}$–25
K. 156 in G:	$11\frac{1}{2}$–$13\frac{1}{2}$	K. 590 in F:	21–28
K. 157 in C:		*String Trio* in E flat, K. 563:	
K. 158 in F:			$38\frac{1}{4}$–44
K. 159 in B flat:		*String Quintets* $(2-2-1)$	
K. 160 in E flat:		K. 406 in C minor:	23
K. 168 in F:	15	K. 515 in C:	$31\frac{1}{2}$
K. 169 in A:		K. 516 in G minor:	$32\frac{1}{2}$–35
K. 170 in C:	14–$16\frac{1}{4}$	K. 593 in D:	$24\frac{1}{2}$–$27\frac{1}{2}$
K. 171 in E flat:		K. 614 in E flat:	21–25
K. 172 in B flat:		*Flute Quartets*	
K. 173 in D minor:	15–18	K. 285 in D:	11–14
K. 387 in G:	23–30	K. 298 in A:	$9\frac{1}{4}$–$11\frac{3}{4}$
K. 421 in D minor:	$23\frac{3}{4}$–28	*Oboe Quartet*	
K. 428 in E flat:	$22\frac{3}{4}$–28	K. 370 in F:	$12\frac{3}{4}$–15
K. 458 in B flat:	22–27	*Clarinet Quintet*	
K. 464 in A:	23–30	K. 581 in A:	26–33
K. 465 in C:	26–$30\frac{1}{2}$	*Piano Quartets*	
K. 499 in D:	$22\frac{1}{2}$–$27\frac{3}{4}$	K. 478 in G minor:	$21\frac{1}{4}$–$26\frac{1}{4}$
K. 575 in D:	$22\frac{1}{4}$–$23\frac{3}{4}$	K. 493 in E flat:	$21\frac{3}{4}$–31

MURRILL
(1909–1952)
Quartet in A minor: 18–$19\frac{3}{4}$

PISTON
(1894–   )
Flute Quintet: 18–$19\frac{3}{4}$.

PROKOVIEV
(1891–   )
Quartet No. 2, Opus 92: 23

RAVEL
(1875–1937)
Quartet in F: $25\frac{1}{2}$–30

RUSSIAN PIECES: LES VENDREDIS

Suite No. 1 for String Quartet
Glazounov, Prelude and Fugue in D minor: $8\frac{1}{2}$–$9\frac{1}{4}$
Artciboucheff, Serenade in A:
Sokolov, Polka in D: 4
Wihtol, Minuet in B flat: 3
Sokolov, Canon in D:
Osten-Sacken, Berceuse in B minor: $2\frac{1}{4}$
Lyadov, Mazurka in D: $2\frac{1}{4}$
Blumenfeld, Sarabande in C minor: $3\frac{1}{2}$
Sokolov, Scherzo in D minor: $6\frac{1}{2}$
Suite No. 2 for String Quartet
Rimsky-Korsakov, Allegro in B flat: $8\frac{1}{2}$–$8\frac{3}{4}$
Lyadov, Sarabande in C minor: $1\frac{1}{4}$
Borodin, Scherzo in D: 11
Lyadov, Fugue in D minor: $2\frac{1}{2}$
Sokolov, Mazurka in A minor:
Glazounov, Courante in G:
Kopylov, Polka in C: 3

SAINT-SAËNS
(1835–1921)
Septet in E flat, Opus 65 (2 – 1 – 1 – Db – Tpt – Piano): 15–$17\frac{1}{2}$

SCHOENBERG
(1874–1951)

Quartets
Opus 7 in D minor: 40–$44\frac{3}{4}$
Opus 10 in F sharp minor: 31
Opus 30: 30–$33\frac{1}{4}$

Opus 37: 31–$33\frac{1}{4}$
String Sextet
Opus 4: *Verklärte Nacht*
    (2 – 2 – 2): $26\frac{1}{2}$–$28\frac{1}{2}$

SCHUBERT
(1797–1828)

Quartets

D. 18 in C minor:

D. 36 in B flat:

D. 46 in C:

D. 68 in B flat:

D. 74 in D:

D. 87 in E flat: $19\frac{1}{2}$–21

D. 94 in D:

D. 112 in B flat: 27–$30\frac{3}{4}$

D. 173 in G minor: $17\frac{3}{4}$–$20\frac{1}{2}$

D. 353 in E: $17\frac{3}{4}$

D. 703 in C minor (*Satz*):
$5\frac{1}{2}$–$8\frac{1}{2}$

D. 804 in A minor: 29–$33\frac{1}{2}$

D. 810 in D minor: 36–$38\frac{1}{2}$

D. 887 in G: $41\frac{1}{2}$–$43\frac{3}{4}$

String Trio in B flat, D. 581: 17

String Quintet in C, D. 956
  (2 – 1 – 2): 45–$55\frac{1}{2}$

Trout Quintet in A, D. 667
  (Piano – 1 – 1 – 1 – Db):
$34\frac{1}{2}$–$38\frac{1}{2}$

Octet in F, D. 803 (2 – 1 –
  1 – Db – Cl – Bn – Hn):
$47\frac{1}{2}$–$57\frac{1}{2}$

SCHUMANN
(1810–1856)

Quartets

Opus 41, No. 1 in A minor: 25

No. 2 in F: 20–22

No. 3 in A: $26\frac{1}{2}$–$28\frac{1}{4}$

Piano Quintet in E flat,
  Opus 44: 27–32

SHOSTAKOVICH
(1906–   )

Quartets

Opus 49 in C: 14–$15\frac{1}{2}$

Opus 69 in A:

Opus 73 in F: $34\frac{3}{4}$

Opus 83 in D: $26\frac{1}{2}$

Opus 92 in B flat:

Opus 101 in G: $28\frac{3}{4}$

Opus 108 in F sharp minor:

Opus 110 in C minor:

Piano Quintet in G minor,
  Opus 57: 28–$33\frac{1}{2}$

SIBELIUS
(1865–1957)

Quartet in D minor, Opus 56 (*Voces Intimae*): $28\frac{1}{4}$–$31\frac{3}{4}$

SMETANA
(1824–1884)

Quartet in E minor, Opus 116 (*From my Life*): $26\frac{1}{2}$–$29\frac{1}{2}$

STRAVINSKY
(1882–   )

Three Pieces for *String Quartet*: *15*

TCHAIKOVSKY
(1840–1893)

Quartet No. 1 in D, Opus 11: $21\frac{1}{2}$–$25\frac{1}{2}$

TURINA
(1882–1949)

Quartet in D minor: *25–27*
La oracion del torero: $8\frac{1}{4}$–$9\frac{1}{4}$

WALTON
(1902–   )

Quartet in A minor: $29\frac{3}{4}$–$30\frac{1}{4}$

WEBERN
(1883–1945)

Five Pieces for *String Quartet*: $12\frac{1}{2}$–$13\frac{1}{4}$

VAUGHAN WILLIAMS
(1872–1958)

Quartet No. 2 in A minor (*For Jean on her birthday*):   *21–25*
Song Cycle, *On Wenlock Edge* (Tenor – 2 – 1 – 1 – piano): $21\frac{1}{2}$–$22\frac{1}{2}$

WOLF
(1860–1903)

Italian Serenade in G (2 – 1 – 1): $6\frac{1}{2}$–8

Index

The principal references to composers and works are clearly shown under 'The Quartets' and 'Timings'. This index only includes additional references.